THE MACMILLAN SHAKESPEARE
ADVISORY EDITOR: PHILIP BROCKBANK
Professor of English and Director of the
Shakespeare Institute, University of Birmingham
GENERAL EDITOR: PETER HOLLINDALE
Senior Lecturer in English and Education,
University of York

KING LEAR

Other titles in the series:

THE MACMILLAN SHAKESPEARE

KING LEAR

Edited by
Philip Edwards

MACMILLAN

First published 1975
Reprinted 1978, 1979, 1980, 1982, 1984 (twice), 1985, 1986, 1989

Published by
MACMILLAN EDUCATION LTD
Houndmills, Basingstoke, Hampshire RG21 2XS
and London
Companies and representatives
throughout the world

Printed in Hong Kong

ISBN 0-333-15588-2

CONTENTS

INTRODUCTION

Shakespeare wrote *King Lear* about 1605, when he was 41. The play comes in the middle of the great series of tragedies which he wrote for his company between 1600 and 1608 – *Hamlet, Othello, King Lear, Macbeth, Antony and Cleopatra, Coriolanus*. His plays on English history, and most of his famous comedies, were behind him. Ahead of him lay the romances, including *The Winter's Tale* and *The Tempest*, before he finished writing for the theatre, around the year 1612. (He died in 1616.)

The story which Shakespeare took for his play was a very old folk-tale of a king and his three daughters, which had been woven into the legendary history of Britain. It was very popular in Tudor times, and was told over and again by chroniclers and poets (including Spenser, who gave a short version of it in *The Faerie Queene*). Towards the end of the sixteenth century there was a play, *The True Chronicle History of King Leir and His Three Daughters* (printed in 1605). Shakespeare knew this old play, and he borrowed from it; but, though he used this and other versions of the tale of King Lear, almost every important feature of his own play is his own addition – the storm, the madness, the Fool, the Gloucester sub-plot, and, above all, the ending. In previous versions, Cordelia successfully restored her father to the throne after defeating the wicked sisters. The old play of *King Leir* ends here. Other versions carry the legend further, to the death of Cordelia. They tell how when Lear died Cordelia became queen. The families of the wicked sisters rose against her and imprisoned her. In prison, she fell into despair and committed suicide (Spenser said she hanged herself). The painful ending of Shakespeare's play, with Cordelia hanged on Edmund's orders and her father dying over her corpse, was Shakespeare's own devising.

I

THE GREATNESS OF KING LEAR

Shakespeare's *King Lear* is one of the most majestic works of literature in English or any other language. It searches and probes the fundamental problems of life: whether there are gods, and whether they care for man; what the relations should be, and what they are, between man and man, between woman and man, between parent and child; what the nature of one's personality is, and how it can be altered; what is true and what is false in the organisation of government and society. It is a story of kings and the fate of kingdoms; of war; of malice and extreme cruelty; of madness, destitution and despair; of deception, adultery and murder – as well as of faith, and love, and loyalty. Its scene is a strange and shadowy pagan Britain, with locations which are, without much definition, the palaces and castles of kings and dukes, barren storm-swept heaths, army camps and battlefields noisy with trumpet calls.

Yet the titanic scope of this play expands from the commonest and simplest of issues, the relations in a family between the young and the old. If we always think about *King Lear* as a play about the warfare of good and evil and the nature of existence, we may miss a lot of what the play has to say to us. It is when we remember it is a play about parents and children, and about the exchange of power as it happens and has to happen everywhere and in every generation as men and women grow old and young people grow up, that we see most clearly into the depths which the play explores. *King Lear* is properly called a universal play: it begins and ends with us in relationships and conflicts which we cannot escape from as long as we call ourselves human; and it places these relationships in such a light that we see ourselves linked to all of mankind, and we see the predicament we are all in, in all its grandeur and all its terror.

It is true of other great plays of Shakespeare, notably

Hamlet and *Antony and Cleopatra*, that the largeness of the design – involving the fate not only of rulers but the states they rule – has for its hub and centre the elementary conditions of the common life of the individual – a son, his father, his uncle, his mother, in *Hamlet*; a woman and her lover in *Antony and Cleopatra*. But in writing *King Lear*, Shakespeare seems to have taken special care to make the current flash backwards and forwards between what is common and what is extraordinary, between what is individual and local and what is general and cosmic. The king of Britain going mad and calling down curses on mankind in the howling storm is an old widower needing to be looked after by his grown-up daughters. The Earl of Gloucester, blinded on a charge of treason, is the same man who chuckled over his escapade with the woman who bore his illegitimate child.

One of the unusual things which Shakespeare has done to create this special texture of *King Lear* is to have a double action, one centred on Lear and his three daughters, and the other on Gloucester and his two sons. Shakespeare got the story of Gloucester from Sir Philip Sidney's popular romance, the *Arcadia*. It is best not to talk of a sub-plot, because the characters of the sub-plot, Gloucester, Edmund and Edgar, are essential characters in the main plot. The parallels between the two actions are close. Each of the two fathers banishes the child who in fact loves him most. Edmund intrigues to supersede and dispossess his father as Goneril and Regan do. He does all he can to cut out his brother as they their sister. Gloucester learns in the pain of physical suffering that he has been deceived about the affection of Edgar as Lear realises in the pain of mental suffering that he has wronged Cordelia.

The differences between the two actions are sufficient to prevent a feeling of mere repetition, and indeed help us to recognise the essential identity of the two stories. We see the common centre the more vividly when Edgar says of Lear, 'He childed as I fathered' (III. 6. 109). Both stories are of parental hastiness and blindness, youthful selfishness

3

and callousness, and a rescue of the old by a rejected child. The cruelty of the father to the child leads to the cruelty of a child to the father; but out of this cruelty the erring father learns the true meaning of natural affection.

So, by giving the story of two individual families, extraordinarily similar but not quite the same, Shakespeare stresses the inner meaning of the stories, and generalises his theme. The Lear story is not unique and unrepeatable; it happens twice. Not only do we understand its significance better, but we are more alarmed by what is happening. Something unexpected, monstrous and hateful is going on, and it is not an isolated accident. We ask ourselves as the characters ask each other, Is some new and horrible way of life coming to us?

The double action of the play is therefore one of the measures which Shakespeare adopted to establish the huge range of *King Lear*, from its insistence on the intensity of individual experience to its philosophic questionings of the meaning of existence. Another measure, which is harder to define, is assisted by the double action. *King Lear* is a 'passion' more than an action so far as Lear and Gloucester are concerned. Hamlet debates, schemes, and tries to carry out revenge; Othello murders his wife; Macbeth murders Duncan; Coriolanus leads an army against his own city. But in *King Lear*, after the two rash actions of the leading characters, Lear banishing Cordelia and Gloucester dispossessing Edgar, we watch the two men suffering the consequences of their actions. As they suffer, they question the meaning of the situation they find themselves in. So Lear: 'Then let them anatomise Regan; see what breeds about her heart. Is there any cause in nature that makes these hard hearts?' (III. 6. 77–8). The great scenes which make up most of Acts Three and Four are reflective scenes in which men are driven by the bitterness of what they are going through to ponder on 'the mystery of things'. These scenes, in which Lear, the Fool, Edgar, Kent and Gloucester are the chief participants, are as far away from realistic drama as anything Shakespeare wrote outside *A Mid-summer Night's Dream* or *The Tempest*. The settings are vague in the extreme – some place or other, outdoors or indoors – and the voices of mad king, supposed beggar, court jester, blind earl and disguised earl create a strange chorus of inquiry and comment which seems to belong more to dream than to waking life. Certainly, all these people belong to a play where a fierce and developing action is being fought, and everything they do and say belongs quite naturally to the unpleasant situations which they find themselves in. But the genius of Shakespeare transfigures them in these magnificent central scenes into the characters of a dream play acting out a symbolic drama in which the riddles of existence are debated. Thus the particular is made universal.

CAN KING LEAR BE ACTED?

To talk in these terms may seem to liken Shakespeare's play to a poetic drama like Shelley's *Prometheus Unbound* or at least to a play very difficult to stage, like Ibsen's last play, *When We Dead Awaken* (which ends with the hero and the heroine hurtling to their death in an avalanche). These central scenes of storm and madness in *King Lear* have provoked a long-continuing debate about whether the play can in fact be acted. In the early nineteenth century, Charles Lamb was firmly convinced that 'the Lear of Shakespeare cannot be acted', that 'to see an old man tottering about the stage with a walking stick' was as nothing compared with what the imagination of a reader of the play could provide. Well, Shakespeare certainly wrote the play to be acted. The company which he wrote it for, usually playing at the Globe Theatre on the south bank of the Thames, acted it at the royal palace of Whitehall before their patron, King James I, on St Stephen's night (the day after Christmas Day) in 1606. They had little in the way of scenery, lighting, or sound effects to help them through their storm-scenes. Perhaps the lack of mechanical aids was their greatest advantage. Harley Granville Barker, an experienced dramatist and director, argued in his *Preface to King Lear* (1927) that actors *can* carry the play on the stage, if they will rely on Shakespeare's strongest weapon, 'the weapon of dramatic poetry'. In these days of electronics, it is difficult to test Granville Barker's theory because the noises provided to present the convulsion of the elements usually prevent the poetry from being fully audible. Not many modern theatregoers are given the chance of understanding the discussion between Kent and the Gentleman in III. 1.

King Lear as a stage-play is pre-eminently the progress of Lear from his first tempestuous anger at Cordelia's lack of co-operation, to his exit into the storm, and then his later reconciliation with Cordelia and the final death-scene. All this material, magnificent for a reader, is even more moving, tense and magnificent on the stage. Time and again, however, the big scenes in Act Three are a disappointment in the theatre, and it is hard not to agree with A. C. Bradley that '*King Lear* is too huge for the stage.' In his *Shakespearean Tragedy* (1904), Bradley argued that 'the vastness of the convulsion both of nature and of human passion' not only could not reveal itself on the stage but was actually denied by what is seen and heard in the theatre. There is no doubt that Shakespeare took a tremendous risk in creating the storm scenes of *King Lear*. The orchestration demands an almost superhuman brilliance from the main performers, Lear, the Fool, and Edgar. We must take leave of Bradley, however, over his opinion that strictly *King Lear* is not a drama at all. There can be no disputing that the central scenes of Lear were conceived in terms of theatre: they are physical three-dimensional images to be presented live and witnessed live. They make no sense except as drama. The debate is, simply, whether any team of actors can quite bring off the gigantic task which Shakespeare has set them.

Earlier generations found both the blinding of Gloucester

and the final scene too much for the stage. Everyone now disagrees. The savagery of putting out Gloucester's eyes is physically sickening in the theatre. But our shock, our strong emotional reaction, is the means by which our minds take in the enormity of what is happening in the story. It is easy to talk about cruelty and suffering. When we see the blinding of Gloucester in the theatre, we know what it is.

The final entry of Lear, with Cordelia dead in his arms, is a stage experience so powerfully moving that it is a desecration to try to describe it. But for 150 years theatregoers were denied this great experience. Unhappiness of this order was too much for the sensibilities of the late seventeenth century. In 1681, Nahum Tate rewrote Shakespeare's play, leaving Cordelia and Lear in triumph at the end. This travesty of Shakespeare's work was not ousted from the stage until the mid-nineteenth century.

LEAR'S MISTAKE

As I have indicated, we have to think of Lear as a king, as a father, and as a man. *King Lear* is a political play, a play about the family, and a play about the nature of man. There is no doubt that in the political realm, the eighty-year-old king had something of a problem about the succession. He had no son, and the youngest of his three daughters, whom he loved most, did not yet have the protection of a husband. There is something to be said for Lear's determination to lay down how the country was to be ruled on his decease. During the whole of Elizabeth's lifetime, Englishmen had worried about the uncertainty of the succession, fearing that the kingdom would become the battleground of rival claimants. Lear announces his plans 'that future strife may be prevented now' (I. 1. 45–6). But his solution of the problem is politically crazy. To the people of Shakespeare's time, brought up under the Tudors to think that the unity

7

of the nation under single rule was one of the most important things on earth, the division of a country into three would have seemed a sure recipe for disaster. Civil war was a deep-seated fear in the folk-memory of Englishmen, whose fore-fathers had suffered the anarchy of the Wars of the Roses. Many plays of the time dealt with the dissensions caused by divided rule. Setting up two powers in a kingdom leads inevitably to the rumours of rivalry and impending war between Cornwall and Albany (e.g. II. 1. 10-11; III. 1. 19-21). Only the common enemy of France holds them together.

The division of the kingdom is an act of political folly, and Lear's abdication is an act of irresponsibility. A king in a hereditary monarchy was felt to be a very special kind of being, and when he was anointed with holy oil at his coronation he became the deputy of God in the country he ruled. It was not open to him to retire. God would 'retire' him when He wished. These Elizabethan ideas are not basically affected by Shakespeare's consciousness that Lear was king in a pagan Britain. The idea of serving out the time which God allots to a man is strongly enforced in the Gloucester story, and summed up in the great words of Edgar, arguing that a man is not free to choose his moment of exit any more than he is to choose his moment of birth.

> Men must endure
> Their going hence, even as their coming hither.
>
> (V. 2. 9-10)

Lear commits a crime of absurdity in un-creating himself as king. Not only that, but he supposes that, while getting rid of the cares of office, he can retain the title of king and all the honour, dignity and obedience that go with it (I. 1. 136). He is proposing a sophisticated way of having your cake and eating it. For kingship was a mysterious unity. Title, dignity, authority, power and responsibilities all belonged together as integral parts of the monarch, and, taken all together, defined his being. You couldn't have one without the other. Lear thought that he could continue to be himself while chopping himself in half.

Though a king was a special kind of being, he was a man, and he was not free from the moral requirements, such as patience, humility and tolerance, imposed on other men. A lifetime of absolute authority seems to have done Lear no good. He has been corrupted by unquestioning obedience to every order, and immediate agreement with every opinion. His pretence of making the divisions of the kingdom according to how eloquently his daughters say they love him is only for the satisfaction of being told in public how marvellous he is (see the note to I. 1. 53). It is this extraordinary vanity which causes all the turmoil and disaster which happen afterwards. For Cordelia won't play. A demand for a public demonstration of affection sets up, in a girl who is deeply fond of her father, a reaction of stubborn refusal. It is a natural enough reaction, and we should not condemn Cordelia too much. Lear's affection for his youngest child, falsely clothing itself in the demand for public protestation, makes Cordelia's affection for him clothe itself in a perverse obstinacy. It is like two magnets getting the wrong way round and repelling each other instead of coming together.

Lear's explosion of wrath against Cordelia and his banishment of her are indefensible. He then has to endure, with the help of the Fool's goading gibes, the understanding of what it is that he has done, in his lack of political wisdom and his emotional rashness. He has deprived himself of power, entrusted his kingdom to two daughters who despise him and care nothing for his welfare, and he has cast out the one who loves him. In doing all this, he has wrecked his own being.

IDENTITY, ROLES AND DISGUISES

What we witness in Lear in those great scenes from I. 4 to
II. 4 is a monumental dislocation of the self. Lear had a fixed
and confident idea of his own being, based on the flattery
and obedience he had received (see IV. 6. 96–105). It was a
false conception. He is too old, proud and inflexible to adjust
himself to a new conception of himself when the former
circumstances change. What cannot bend must break; and
in the end he goes mad. The progress of this shattering of a
man's identity must be one of the most marvellous things
Shakespeare has given us. It starts with a little comic turn
in I. 4: 'Does any here know me? This is not Lear' (l. 227),
but the note becomes tragic fifty lines later when he talks of
his 'frame of nature' being wrenched from its fixed place
(ll. 270–71). He says (as though it were possible!) that he
will 'resume the shape' he has cast off (l. 311). In the
ensuing scenes he wars with the conflicting emotions of
anger, indignation, self-pity, remorse and fear in order to
keep some kind of balance in himself (see the note to II. 4.
220–37). His raging outcry in the storm is the last of the old
being. His lunacy is a kind of temporary personality until
he is born again as though from death when he wakes out of
his deep sleep in the presence of Cordelia, and greets her
with humility and hesitancy.

> Pray do not mock me;
> I am a very foolish fond old man,
> Fourscore and upward . . .

> . . . Do not laugh at me,
> For (as I am a man) I think this lady
> To be my child Cordelia . . .

> You must bear with me. Pray you now,
> forget and forgive; I am old and foolish.
> (IV. 7. 59–85)

These radical changes in Lear's personality, from arrogant and selfish king through the purgatory of lunacy to this humility, occur in a play which dwells more than most of Shakespeare's plays on the way our very nature can change, or seem to change. In Lear's eyes, Goneril and Regan suddenly change from loving daughters to cold-hearted strangers. Gloucester has first to adjust himself to the villainy of Edgar, and then to the more appalling truth of Edmund's villainy. These changes of nature are of course the result of wilful deceit on the part of the villains, but even so they bear witness to the uncertainty of what a man really is. Lear's 'education' in the storm and in his madness is above all in the deceptiveness of what people appear to be, from the 'simular of virtue That art incestuous' (III. 2. 54) to the 'simpering dame' who 'goes to't' with more appetite than the fitchew (IV. 6. 118–23).

The fluidity of what we are is marked by the use of disguise in the play. The Earl of Kent spends most of the play in disguise as a servant, Caius. Edgar assumes one role after another until finally he enters as the Avenging Knight and kills Edmund. In his second personality as Poor Tom he has the profoundest effect on Lear. It is hard for us not to think of Poor Tom as a distinct and 'real' person, and to remember that it is only an acted part. Perhaps Edgar found more 'reality' in his role than he expected to. That Edgar can so completely transfer himself to another identity helps us to see how unfixed our being is. His role in the play – as one who assumes roles – has something rather mysterious in it. He is the person mainly responsible for the major change in temperament in both of the two leading characters, Lear and Gloucester. As Lear stares at Edgar in his disguise as a half-naked lunatic beggar, the reality of what man naturally is, without the artificial additions of civilisation, is borne in upon him. 'Is man no more than this?' he cries (III. 4. 102–3). But what Lear is looking at is not 'the thing itself' (as he calls it) at all; it is an Earl's son acting a part to avoid detection. Edgar practises a more conscious deception on his father; keeping his real identity concealed and acting three assumed roles in turn, he plays on him the extraordinary trick of the false leap over Dover cliff, thus curing him of his resolve to take his own life (IV. 6. 9–80).

At one extreme there are the villains like Goneril, Regan, and Edmund, who can conceal their true identities under masks of obliging friendliness. At the other extreme are people of positive goodness like Kent and Edgar who seem able to help people and bring about good results just as effectively even in the anonymity of disguise. Goodness can conceal itself and work secretly, as evil can.

By choice, or through the pressure of adversity and changing circumstances, people alter out of all recognition in *King Lear*. There is one person in the play whose true identity we feel we never know, and that is the Fool. The Fool can be un-funny in the theatre, and with him we again feel something of the paradox of the acting of *Lear*: the attentive reader gets more of the extraordinary cleverness and subtlety of the Fool's rich nonsense, but he knows that the part can only really come to life on the stage, with a first-class actor singing the snatches of song, winking at the audience, cowering in the storm. Like Feste in *Twelfth Night*, a part which Shakespeare probably wrote for the same actor, Robert Armin, the Fool in *Lear* is a mysterious person. That he loves Lear more than the faithful Kent does, that he loves Cordelia almost as much as Lear does – this we know; that he is the most intelligent person in the play, more intelligent than Edmund, this we know. But his whole part in the play is acting a part, and we must accept that his real personality is a complete enigma to us – as mysterious as his sudden disappearance from the play in III. 6.

LEARNING THROUGH SUFFERING

At the beginning of the play, although we can't help being impressed by the imperious majesty of Lear, we find him a self-absorbed, irascible, obstinate, unwise tyrant. As we watch the change in his nature which we have described, we also see him learning through bitter experience a new valuation of himself and the world. The quarrel in the first and second acts about how many knights Lear should have attending him may seem comic at times, but it is deadly serious to Lear because, until he goes out into the storm, value for him depends on material quantity which you can weigh or number. Love was something to be measured by how many superlatives you could put into a speech, to be rewarded by a corresponding number of square miles of territory. So his personal dignity depends on how quickly people obey him, and how many people he has serving him. When Lear tries to explain his 'true need' for his hundred knights, he gets completely tied up (see notes to II. 4. 262–268). In the wildness of the storm, however, his thoughts begin to turn away from the necessities of prestige to man's real needs, and this is accompanied by a turning away from the needs of self to the needs of others. Lear's sudden awareness of and pity for the homeless and destitute in his prayer – in the drenching rain – for 'poor naked wretches' is one of the supreme moments of the play (III. 4. 28).

This awareness of what 'true need' *really* is, and that he and his kind are 'sophisticated', could not come without the earlier deep insight (III. 2. 49–60) in which Lear first sees through the smooth world of appearances which (in Goneril and Regan) he feels has betrayed him. The storm reveals the wickedness which lies beneath the surface of respectability. Right through until his last mad scene (IV. 6), Lear continues to revalue society, discarding the criteria of wealth, position or respectability. It is a bitter revaluation when he sees in all men an equality in sinful desires, so that

13

'none does offend', because everybody offends (IV. 6. 167).
No one is innocent enough to charge anyone else with guilt.
But the fruit of this dark and disenchanted vision comes
when Lear, sane again and reconciled with Cordelia, is
able to accept defeat and the humiliation of imprisonment
with a positive joy. He knows now whom to trust and how
to love; he can acknowledge his own errors, and disregard
the whole corrupt world of power and position.

> Come, let's away to prison.
> We two alone will sing like birds i'th'cage.
> When thou dost ask me blessing, I'll kneel down
> And ask of thee forgiveness. So we'll live,
> And pray, and sing, and tell old tales, and laugh
> At gilded butterflies, and hear poor rogues
> Talk of court news; and we'll talk with them too –
> Who loses and who wins, who's in, who's out –
> And take upon's the mystery of things,
> As if we were God's spies; and we'll wear out,
> In a walled prison, packs and sects of great ones
> That ebb and flow by th'moon. . . .
> Upon such sacrifices, my Cordelia,
> The gods themselves throw incense. (V. 3. 8–21)

It is this movement through suffering from faulty, self-
regarding, materialistic vision to an unworldly, undeceived,
humble affection which led Bradley to say that this play
should be called *The Redemption of King Lear*. Important
though this purification of Lear's understanding is, it is a
long way from being what the play is 'all about'.

A CONFLICT OF PHILOSOPHIES

Lear is indeed, as he sees himself, 'a man more sinned
against than sinning' (III. 2. 59–60). He does something
shamefully bad, the consequences of which are disastrous.
One of the worst aspects of what he does is that he gives

scope and power to heartless people like Goneril and Regan, just as Gloucester gives scope to Edmund. Lear, for all his faults, does not belong with these people. The play is very much a warfare between two very different kinds of people, having very different views of the world. To some extent, the line between the two armies is the line between youth and age, and we remind ourselves that, partially, *King Lear* is about the conflict of the generations. Lear himself is an archetypal 'father-figure', stern, authoritarian, laying down the law. When a daughter refuses to comply with his orders, he disowns her.

> Better thou
> Hadst not been born than not t' have pleased me better.

When age asserts its rights to be obeyed in this way, we can understand, if not forgive youth when it impatiently shrugs off the ties between child and parent. To Goneril and Regan, Lear is simply a tiresome aged parent who must be reduced to submissiveness. He has (incredibly) given away his power to them, and next they try to take away his self-respect. So that what was for Lear a device for spending his declining days peacefully, becomes the occasion for a frightening struggle for survival against a new generation which sees him as obsolete and is impatient to succeed him. The clash between the two generations is very clearly shown in the beginning of the sub-plot, when Gloucester fussily laments that the world is going to the dogs – 'We have seen the best of our time' (I. 2. 116–17); and his son laughs contemptuously at the superstitions of old age.

On the one side are the older generation: Lear, Gloucester, Kent. On the other side, youth: Edmund, Cornwall, Goneril, Regan. Lear, Gloucester and Kent accept a world of traditional authority and hierarchy, of service, respect and obedience, in the state and in the family. The world is meaningless to them without the mutual ties of obligation between lord and liegeman, parent and child. Lear and Gloucester are one-sided in their early views about the bonds of natural affection. Lear is constantly looking for gratitude (see the note to III. 4. 15–16) and thinks of what is due to him more than what he owes to others. Because they are complacent in never questioning the status quo, they tend to be overbearing and demanding, and to be hasty and hot-tempered when the outward signs of duty are not present. And so it is they, the upholders of the ancient beliefs in loyalty and the bonds of affection, which they see as the *natural* bonds of society and the family, who actually disrupt and sever those ties by outlawing first Cordelia and then Edgar. Kent's swift and courageous rebuke of his master Lear shows his dedication to the ideals of feudal and family concord and his horror at Lear's overturning them. He devotes the rest of his life to trying to repair the damage which Lear has done.

On the other side, Edmund is the characteristic Shakespearean villain, like Iago and Richard III, brisk, alert, intelligent and witty, keen to sweep away the cobwebs of tradition, ceremony, convention and superstition. In his splendid introduction to us in I. 2, he presents himself remarkably as a modernist. A man is in charge of his own fortunes, and must not be encumbered and restrained by the old pieties and outworn beliefs. All the young people opposing Gloucester and Lear are realists, questioning received morality, and if anyone is tempted to congratulate them on this, he soon stops short, in the face of their total selfishness and absolute callousness. Progressive they may be, but they are quite clear that in order to move forward it is necessary to stand up for oneself, at whatever cost to others.

Goneril and Regan are indifferent to what may happen to the aged Lear in the storm. It is his own look-out, they say. Gloucester attempts to bring succour to him; Edmund betrays his father to Cornwall, and Gloucester loses his eyes as an alleged traitor. After this climax of treachery and cruelty it is the turn of young people of a very different order, the rejected Cordelia and Edgar, to rescue the old, cherish them and re-establish the values of the relationship which the old had so imperfectly and erratically upheld. The love of Edgar and Cordelia for their parents is not much spoken of in the play, but it is the rock on which the play is built. Like Kent, they do not demand as the price of their love that those they love should always behave as they would wish them to; they are incapable of removing their affection because of a moral disapproval. This is the love which Shakespeare spoke of in his Sonnet 116:

> Love is not love
> Which alters when it alteration finds,
> Or bends with the remover to remove.
> O no, it is an ever-fixéd mark
> That looks on tempests and is never shaken.

Cordelia comes back to England to save her father, by warfare if necessary, from the inhumanity of her sisters. In the scene of reunion between Lear and Cordelia is all the justification that needs to be made for the concept of a bond between parent and child. This bond now carries with it no thought of hierarchy, no obedient display of gratitude. It is a simple matter of two people recognising that they love and need one another.

> When thou dost ask me blessing, I'll kneel down
> And ask of thee forgiveness.

On the one side, father and daughter have been drawn together by the mutual link which all the injustice which he did to her could not break. The other side are victorious in the war, but nothing can keep together those who have denied the traditional bonds which cement social relationships. They are fragmented by their dissensions and rivalries, shown most clearly in the murderous sexual rivalry of Goneril and Regan for the person of Edmund.

In this story of faulty old people, attacked and pursued by the emancipated and uncaring young, and then championed and rescued by a faithful and constant child, we feel that more is suggested than a warfare between philosophies or a warfare between the generations. *King Lear* can be seen as a play about the fight for survival of an old world of service and loyalty against a cold-hearted and self-seeking progressiveness. Shakespeare's tragedies take much of their power from his sense of the tension between an old world dying and a new one being born. Though he seems to have little enthusiasm for the 'modern' world, represented by Edmund in *Lear*, Claudius in *Hamlet*, Caesar in *Antony and Cleopatra*, he does not look at the old feudal values through rose-coloured spectacles. What the rescue of the old by the faithful young seems to suggest is some new faith in which the energy of the young re-invigorates rather than rejects the past. But the ending of *King Lear* presents it as a lost cause.

THE PATTERN OF KING LEAR

When Edgar finally reveals himself to his blinded father, Gloucester dies of a heart attack. Lear and Cordelia have no time at all together in their new-found happiness. Whatever it is that is affirmed when the child re-cements the relationship which the father had broken, death comes so quickly that nothing can be built up.

King Lear seems to be fashioned out of irony and paradox. The ceremony which Lear devised to show his love for his youngest child becomes the occasion for disowning her. Lear learns of the untrustworthiness of Goneril and Regan only after he has given his kingdom to them. The blinded Gloucester says, 'I stumbled when I saw': he sees more clearly when he is blind. Lear behaved madly when he was sane, and understands things much better when he is mad. Albany says of Cordelia, 'The gods defend her!', and immediately Lear enters with Cordelia dead in his arms. When Kent, who has worked during the whole of the play to bring Cordelia and Lear together again – 'that full issue For which I razed my likeness' (I. 4. 3-4) – finally comes to reveal himself to his master, both he and Lear are near death, and Cordelia is dead. His long-hoped-for explanation falls on deaf ears. Is this the promised end?

Kent's phrase, 'Is this the promised end?', as Lear comes on for the last time, carrying his dead daughter, echoes with meaning. It reflects his bitter sense of the irony of what has been achieved. Lear and Cordelia *are* together again – but she is dead. In another sense, the promised end is what Edgar understands Kent to mean, the end of the world, the last trump and the last judgement. In a third sense, Kent is asking if all this unhappiness is a conclusion which has been arranged for man by the gods, 'Is all that we hope for out of life answered with this?'

How far do we feel that events in *King Lear* are dictated by a higher power? It is very noticeable that the gods are continuously being mentioned and appealed to in *King Lear*. Lear invokes 'the sacred radiance of the sun' and the influence of the heavens 'From whom we do exist and cease to be.' He swears by Apollo and Hecate and Jupiter, and calls on the goddess Nature herself. Gloucester is a superstitious believer in astrology. Edmund addresses a goddess Nature, but by Nature *he* means doing whatever you feel like. (An important book by W. R. Elton, '*King Lear*' *and the Gods*, shows how carefully Shakespeare set each one of his characters in his pagan play in an individual relationship with the gods, and how, especially in Lear, that relationship changed as circumstances changed.) When the difficulties in the play multiply, everyone turns to the question of how far the gods are involved in what is happening. Have they caused it? Will they allow it? 'If you yourselves are old,' says Lear, 'Make it your cause. Send down and take my part!' (II. 4. 189-90). Or again, 'If it be you that stirs these daughters' hearts/Against their father . . .' (II. 4. 272-3).

After he has been blinded, Gloucester turns bitterly against the gods:

> As flies to wanton boys are we to th' gods;
> They kill us for their sport. (IV. 1. 36–7)

But his son believes that suffering is divine punishment.
'The gods are just,' Edgar proclaims to the defeated
Edmund concerning their father,

> The dark and vicious place where thee he got
> Cost him his eyes. (V. 3. 171–2)

Albany is quick to interpret Cornwall's death as the
vengeance of heaven. But, as we have seen, his cry, 'The
gods defend her!' is answered immediately by Lear's entry
with the dead girl.

In the strange rapture of his speech to Cordelia as they
are led away to prison, Lear feels the nearness of the gods
more directly than anywhere else in the play. He no longer
appeals to them to come and smite his enemies. In defeat
and dispossession, he has gained something worth all the
world, Cordelia, and he feels that renunciation of the world,
in the company of Cordelia, puts him in tune with a trans-
cendent order of values. In his relationship with Cordelia
he has found a truth from which he can never turn away.

> He that parts us shall bring a brand from heaven
> And fire us hence like foxes.

The next time we see him, his daughter has been murdered.
Lear makes no attempt in his last speeches to relate what has
happened to the will of the gods. He can only ask the
question,

> Why should a dog, a horse, a rat have life
> And thou no breath at all?

How far the gods care, how far they are responsible, is never
answered in the play. All the invocations and the questions,
all the attempts at interpreting, only deepen the sense of
mystery over what controls human destiny. The one thing
that is certain is that men are not in control of their own
fates.

Yet, for all the lack of 'answers' in *King Lear*, it does not strike us that Shakespeare portrays an absurd world of meaningless and unrelated happenings. If men are not in control of their fates, what they do has the closest links with what happens to them. Wheels *do* come full circle – but never as men expect them to, and never in a way that is consistent with an explicable system of divine providence. Perhaps the most extraordinary and uncomfortable pair of speeches in the play are those of the two brothers in Act Five, which I have already quoted in part.

> EDGAR My name is Edgar, and thy father's son.
> The gods are just, and of our pleasant vices
> Make instruments to plague us:
> The dark and vicious place where thee he got
> Cost him his eyes.
> EDMUND   Th' hast spoken right, 'tis true.
> The wheel is come full circle; I am here.
>
> (V. 3. 168–73)

How can we understand this last line of Edmund's? It is not Fortune's wheel he is talking about, but a complete cycle which began with his begetting and ends with his death. The subsidiary action of *King Lear* begins with Gloucester's flippancy about the 'good sport' when Edmund was conceived out of wedlock. That son betrayed him and caused his blinding, and, by thus provoking the vengeance of Edgar, brought upon himself his own death. While Edgar's view that Gloucester's blindness shows the justice of the gods is his own, there is no doubt about the chain of events from the conception of the illegitimate child to the death of both father and child. The adultery of Gloucester is always being mentioned in the play (see note to I. 2. 133).

Shakespeare is not making the point that men will not suffer if they remain faithful to their wives. In the depths of his insane perceptions, Lear sees all sexual rectitude, all moral restraint, as futile, for his daughters, lawfully begotten, have turned against him and sought his death. 'Let copulation thrive!' he cries, for the family bond which sexual fidelity creates has no meaning. No, it is not adultery that is the 'cause' of Gloucester's catastrophe. In some sense, it is sexual pleasure itself. For it is hard to ignore Lear's own sense of guilt about the begetting of his daughters and Poor Tom's obscene reply:

> LEAR Judicious punishment! 'Twas this flesh begot
> Those pelican daughters.
> EDGAR Pillicock sat on Pillicock Hill.   (III. 4. 73–5)

These hints about the relationship of the sexual act with what men later suffer from their children have an allegorical force. They help to suggest to us as we witness *King Lear* a world in which there is no escape from the consequences of everything we do. The most horrifying thing about the final entry of Lear with Cordelia dead in his arms is that *he* killed her – he and Gloucester. The wheel has come full circle and she is there. He banished her and gave power to Goneril and Regan. Gloucester gave power to Edmund. From there every step is related to the one after until the devastating conclusion. All, that is, except one, the most important one, the murder of Cordelia. If Edmund had acted more quickly, if Albany and the others had been more conscious of the absence of Lear and Cordelia, she might have been saved. It seems she dies because of absence of mind, and muddle. Her death is indeed another of the ironies of the play. It is part of the remorseless scheme of things that Edmund should command her murder; but she might have been saved, if the ceremonial completion of other issues had not preoccupied people's minds.

This element, almost of chance, darkens the atmosphere at the end of the play. It is bad enough that we can trace the catastrophe back not only to the unprincipled ambitions of cruel people but to the unthinking deeds of comparatively good people, even the intransigence of Cordelia herself, but it is worse that the final blow of the hanging of Cordelia should depend on forgetfulness.

There is another side to the weight of human responsibility which a play like *King Lear* so heavily burdens us with. And that is the sense of the lifting of the burden which recognition of responsibility and regret for misdeeds bring. Lear admits the wrong he has done, and asks Cordelia forgiveness; and he does not think it enough to ask once only. What comfort there is in *King Lear* exists in that short period when Lear and Cordelia are together in love and mutual forgiveness. Their new relationship, briefly seized out of disaster, was something very important to Shakespeare, because we see him returning to the theme of the discovery of real affection between father and daughter in several plays which he wrote after this: *Pericles*, *The Winter's Tale* and *The Tempest*. It is a kind of solution to the problem of the generations. The young forgive the old and the old rely on the young. It is not exactly a 'way of life', with Cordelia dead and Lear dying, but such an affection between two people, so dearly bought, provides a moment of vision for us as well as for them, and does something to offset the grimness of the rest of what we have seen.

A NOTE ON THE TEXT

The text of *King Lear* has come down to us in two rather different versions, which we call the Quarto and the Folio (referring to the format of the original publications). The Quarto was published in 1608. Although it contains 300 lines not found in the Folio, it was not printed from Shakespeare's manuscript and was probably an unauthorised text. Much of it is garbled and unintelligible, and prose and verse are mixed up. How this text was got together we do not know. The Folio text was printed in the 'first Folio' of 1623. This was the collected edition of Shakespeare's plays brought out by the fellow-members of his theatre-company after his death. The Folio text of *King Lear* contains 100 lines not found in the Quarto; the 300 lines which it lacks are probably acting-cuts. There seems no doubt that the Folio text represents an official manuscript of Shakespeare's play. But, instead of working direct from this manuscript, the printers of the Folio must have decided to work with an old copy of the Quarto text, laboriously altered to bring it into line with the authorised manuscript. This task was not perfectly carried out, so that the Folio often repeats the Quarto's errors. Sometimes, when the Folio text differs from the Quarto, we can still believe that the early, un-authorised Quarto has the better reading, nearer to Shakespeare's own words, which, for one reason or another, have been weakened or corrupted on their way to the Folio text.

Although the text of this edition is based firmly on the more authoritative Folio text, there are quite a number of occasions when a reading from the Quarto has been pre-ferred. A few examples follow.

	Quarto	Folio
I. 1. 150	stoops	falls
II. 1. 8	ear-bussing	ear-kissing
II. 1. 76	spurs	spirits
II. 2. 76	Bring	Being
II. 4. 298	bleak	high
III. 7. 57	rash	stick
IV. 4. 18	distress	desires
IV. 6. 71	enridgèd	enraged
IV. 6. 83	coining	crying

In IV. 7 the staging of the 'discovery' of Lear as it is implied by the Quarto is preferred, as probably nearer to what was originally acted on Shakespeare's stage, to the staging of the Folio, where the sleeping Lear is carried on to the stage in a chair (see note to IV. 7. 25).

THE CHARACTERS

LEAR, King of Britain
GONERIL, his eldest daughter
REGAN, his second daughter
CORDELIA, his youngest daughter
DUKE OF ALBANY, Goneril's husband
DUKE OF CORNWALL, Regan's husband
KING OF FRANCE, Cordelia's suitor, later her husband
DUKE OF BURGUNDY, Cordelia's suitor
EARL OF KENT
EARL OF GLOUCESTER
EDGAR, Gloucester's son
EDMUND, Gloucester's bastard son
Lear's FOOL
OSWALD, Goneril's steward
CURAN, a courtier
OLD MAN, Gloucester's tenant
DOCTOR
HERALD
CAPTAIN, serving Edmund
KNIGHT, following Lear

Knights of Lear's train, Gentlemen, Attendants, Soldiers, Servants

KING LEAR

ACT ONE, scene 1

The play opens in the royal palace, where two leading noble-men are waiting for the all-important ceremony in which King Lear is to resign his royal authority to his three daughters, and arrange the betrothal of the youngest of them, Cordelia.

[1] had more affected *was fonder of*

[5-7] equalities . . . moiety *the shares are so alike that neither Duke, however particular, can prefer the other's portion. Lear has already decided how much of the kingdom each of his daughters is to get.*

[9] breeding *upbringing*

[11] brazed *hardened*
[12] conceive *understand*
[13] could *could conceive*

[17] issue *product (Edmund)*
[18] proper *handsome*
[19] son . . . by order of law *legitimate son*

[24] whoreson *fellow. Like 'knave', the term is used with rough affection.*

[30] sue *beg*
[31] study deserving *work to deserve Kent's regard*

ACT ONE

Scene 1. *Enter* KENT, GLOUCESTER *and* EDMUND

KENT I thought the king had more affected the
Duke of Albany than Cornwall.

GLOUCESTER It did always seem so to us; but now in
the division of the kingdom it appears not which of
the dukes he values most, for equalities are so
weighed that curiosity in neither can make choice
of either's moiety.

KENT Is not this your son, my lord?

GLOUCESTER His breeding, sir, hath been at my charge.
I have so often blushed to acknowledge him that   10
now I am brazed to 't.

KENT I cannot conceive you.

GLOUCESTER Sir, this young fellow's mother could;
whereupon she grew round-wombed, and had
indeed, sir, a son for her cradle ere she had a husband
for her bed. Do you smell a fault?

KENT I cannot wish the fault undone, the issue of it
being so proper.

GLOUCESTER But I have a son, sir, by order of law,
some year elder than this, who yet is no dearer in   20
my account. Though this knave came something
saucily to the world before he was sent for, yet was
his mother fair; there was good sport at his making,
and the whoreson must be acknowledged. Do you
know this noble gentleman, Edmund?

EDMUND No, my lord.

GLOUCESTER My lord of Kent. Remember him here-
after as my honourable friend.

EDMUND My services to your lordship.

KENT I must love you, and sue to know you better.   30

EDMUND Sir, I shall study deserving.

29

[32] out *abroad*

Sennet *processional fanfare*

coronet *symbol of Lear's regal power; see ll. 136–140*

[34] Attend *act as escort to*

[Edmund] *It is traditional for Edmund to leave at this point, though there is no exit for him in the original texts. He has to re-appear in I. 2 as though in another part of the country. It might be a good idea to have him on stage until l. 126 or 268.*

[37] Meantime . . . darker purpose *while we are waiting for France and Burgundy (and the happy business of the betrothal of Cordelia), I shall announce the graver side of what I have in mind to do (the division of the kingdom)*

[39] fast *firm*

[44] constant will to publish *fixed determination to make known*

[45] several dowers *individual marriage portions*

future strife *see Introduction, page 7*

[46] prevented *forestalled*

[48] sojourn *visit*

[51] Interest *legal possession*

[53] our largest bounty *Since the divisions have already been made and are known (see ll. 3–6), everyone must recognise this bid for the largest share as a charade. It would seem that the biggest portion has already been marked out for Cordelia.*

[54] Where nature . . . challenge *to the person whose natural affection and personal desert make the strongest claim; or to the person whose natural affection is as great as ('challenges') her personal desert.*

[56] wield *handle*

[57] space and liberty *room to move about and freedom to do so*

GLOUCESTER He hath been out nine years, and away he
shall again. The king is coming.

Sennet. Enter one bearing a coronet, then KING
LEAR, CORNWALL, ALBANY, GONERIL, REGAN,
CORDELIA *and* ATTENDANTS

LEAR Attend the lords of France and Burgundy,
Gloucester.

GLOUCESTER I shall, my liege.

[*Exeunt* GLOUCESTER *and* EDMUND

LEAR Meantime we shall express our darker purpose. *more serious*
Give me the map there. Know that we have
divided *he is King*
In three our kingdom; and 'tis our fast intent
To shake all cares and business from our age, 40
Conferring them on younger strengths while we
Unburdened crawl toward death. Our son of *poetry used in formal speech*
Cornwall,
And you our no less loving son of Albany,
We have this hour a constant will to publish
Our daughters' several dowers, that future strife
May be prevented now. The princes, France and *Giving Kingdom up because of age*
Burgundy,
Great rivals in our youngest daughter's love,
Long in our court have made their amorous
sojourn,
And here are to be answered. Tell me, my
daughters
(Since now we will divest us both of rule, 50
Interest of territory, cares of state),
Which of you shall we say doth love us most,
That we our largest bounty may extend
Where nature doth with merit challenge. Goneril,
Our eldest-born, speak first.

GONERIL Sir, I love you more than word can wield
the matter,
Dearer than eyesight, space and liberty,

[61] breath *speech*
    unable *incompetent*
[62] all manner of 'so much' *all kind of comparison*

[64] bounds *territories*
[65] champains *open country*
    riched *enriched*
[66] wide-skirted meads *broad meadows*
[67] issues *descendants*
[68] perpetual *for all time*
[70] self mettle *same spirit*
[71] prize . . . worth *assess myself at her value*
[72] names . . . love *describes exactly the way my love works*

[75] square of sense *properly proportioned feelings*
[76] felicitate *made happy*

[79] More ponderous *of more weight*

[82 validity *value*

[84] least *in public importance*
[85] vines . . . milk *This conveys a sense of richness rather than describes the agriculture. See the Song of Solomon, 5:1.*
[86] interested *related*

[91] Nothing . . . nothing *A common proverb: in Latin 'Ex nihilo nihil fit.'*

Beyond what can be valued rich or rare,
No less than life, with grace, health, beauty,
   honour,
As much as child e'er loved, or father found;   60
A love that makes breath poor, and speech unable;
Beyond all manner of 'so much' I love you.

CORDELIA [*Aside*] What shall Cordelia speak? Love
   and be silent.

LEAR Of all these bounds, even from this line to this,
With shadowy forests and with champains riched,
With plenteous rivers and wide-skirted meads,
We make thee lady. To thine and Albany's issues
Be this perpetual. What says our second daughter,
Our dearest Regan, wife of Cornwall?

REGAN I am made of that self mettle as my sister,   70
And prize me at her worth. In my true heart
I find she names my very deed of love:
Only she comes too short, that I profess
Myself an enemy to all other joys
Which the most precious square of sense possesses,
And find I am alone felicitate
In your dear highness' love.

CORDELIA [*Aside*]   Then poor Cordelia!
   And yet not so, since I am sure my love's
   More ponderous than my tongue.

LEAR To thee and thine, hereditary ever,
Remain this ample third of our fair kingdom,   80
No less in space, validity, and pleasure
Than that conferred on Goneril. Now, our joy,
Although our last and least, to whose young love
The vines of France and milk of Burgundy
Strive to be interessed, what can you say to draw
A third more opulent than your sisters'? Speak.

CORDELIA Nothing, my lord.

LEAR Nothing?

CORDELIA Nothing.   90

LEAR Nothing will come of nothing; speak again.

[Handwritten annotations in right margin: "The daughters exaggerated praise makes Lear suspicious of their true motives"]

[Handwritten annotation: "My love has more weight than my words"]

33

[94] According to my bond   *as I am in duty bound as a daughter and a subject*

[98] as are right fit   *as it is proper they should be returned*

[101] Haply when I   *when I, it may be,*
[102] plight   *marriage-pledge*

[110–13] For by . . . to be   *Lear is here established as a pious pagan, acknowledging his dependence on non-Christian powers.*
[111] Hecate   *goddess of the world of spirits*
[112] operation of the orbs   *influences of the planets, etc.*
[113] From whom we do exist   *by virtue of which we come into existence*
[115] Propinquity . . . blood   *nearness of relationship and sharing of blood-tie*
[117] this   *his heart(?)*
   Scythian   *inhabitant of what is now Russia; supposedly cruel and savage*
[118] generation   *offspring*
   messes   *dishes of food*
[121] liege   *person to whom one owes allegiance*
[123] Come . . . wrath   *do not try to separate me from my anger*
   dragon   *emblem of the ancient British monarchy, symbolic of the king's stern power*

CORDELIA Unhappy that I am, I cannot heave
  My heart into my mouth. I love your majesty
  According to my bond, no more nor less.

not very affectionate

LEAR How, how, Cordelia? Mend your speech a little,
  Lest you may mar your fortunes.

CORDELIA   Good my lord,
  You have begot me, bred me, loved me. I
  Return those duties back as are right fit,
  Obey you, love you, and most honour you.
  Why have my sisters husbands, if they say   100
  They love you all? Haply when I shall wed,
  That lord whose hand must take my plight shall
    carry
  Half my love with him, half my care and duty.
  Sure I shall never marry like my sisters,
  To love my father all.

LEAR But goes thy heart with this?

CORDELIA   Ay, my good lord.

LEAR So young, and so untender?

CORDELIA So young, my lord, and true.

LEAR Let it be so, thy truth then be thy dower.
  For by the sacred radiance of the sun,   110
  The mysteries of Hecate and the night,
  By all the operation of the orbs
  From whom we do exist and cease to be,
  Here I disclaim all my paternal care,
  Propinquity and property of blood,
  And as a stranger to my heart and me
  Hold thee from this for ever. The barbarous
    Scythian,
  Or he that makes his generation messes
  To gorge his appetite, shall to my bosom
  Be as well neighboured, pitied, and relieved,   120
  As thou my sometime daughter.

Lear disowns her

KENT   Good my liege –

LEAR Peace, Kent!
  Come not between the dragon and his wrath.

[124] set my rest *venture my all (from the card game of primero)* and *fix my repose*

[125] kind nursery *affectionate care*

Hence . . . sight! *To Kent or to Cordelia? Neither of them goes.*

avoid *get out of*

[126] So . . . peace as *as I wish to find peace in the grave, so . . .*

[126–7] here . . . from her *This curious phrase is a carry-over from Lear's intention to give away his daughter in marriage.*

[127] Who stirs? *The attendants are dazed by what is happening.*

[129] digest *assimilate*

[130] marry her *be the dowry to win her a husband*

[132–3] large . . . majesty *great accompaniments of kingship*

[134] reservation *a legal term for a claim to a right*

[137] all th' addition *all the titles and designation*

[138] execution of the rest *carrying out of all remaining authority*

[140] part *share*

[144] The bow . . . drawn *Lear is determined on his course*

make . . . shaft *keep out of the way of the arrow*

[145] fork *arrow-head*

[147] thou *A subject would not normally use 'thou' to his king.*

[150] Reserve thy state *retain your king-like qualities*

[152] Answer . . . judgement *I will back my opinions with my life*

I loved her most, and thought to set my rest
On her kind nursery. Hence, and avoid my sight!
So be my grave my peace as here I give
Her father's heart from her. Call France! Who
    stirs?
Call Burgundy! Cornwall and Albany,
With my two daughters' dowers digest the third;
Let pride, which she calls plainness, marry her.   130
I do invest you jointly with my power,
Pre-eminence, and all the large effects
That troop with majesty. Ourself by monthly
    course,
With reservation of an hundred knights
By you to be sustained, shall our abode
Make with you by due turn. Only we shall retain
The name and all th' addition to a king: the sway,
Revenue, execution of the rest,
Belovéd sons, be yours; which to confirm,
This coronet part between you.

KENT   Royal Lear,   140
Whom I have ever honoured as my king,
Loved as my father, as my master followed,
As my great patron thought on in my prayers –
LEAR The bow is bent and drawn, make from the
    shaft.
KENT Let it fall rather, though the fork invade
The region of my heart! Be Kent unmannerly
When Lear is mad. What wouldst thou do, old
    man?
Think'st thou that duty shall have dread to speak
When power to flattery bows? To plainness
    honour's bound
When majesty stoops to folly. Reserve thy state,   150
And in thy best consideration check
This hideous rashness. Answer my life my
    judgement,
Thy youngest daughter does not love thee least,

Kent attempts to calm Lear and make him think over his action

[155] Reverb no hollowness   *are not made louder by the (echoing) hollowness of their hearts*

[156–7] pawn . . . wage   *(1) mere chess-piece to be used in contest, or (2) stake to wager*

[160] blank   *centre of target*

[161] Apollo   *god of the sun*

[162] vassal   *lowly dependent*
miscreant   *unbeliever (because of Kent's contemptuous reference to ' thy gods')*

[165] the foul disease   *i.e. those who may kill you*

[166] vent clamour   *utter a noise*

[167] recreant   *traitor*

[169] That   *because*

[170] strained   *excessive*

[171] betwixt . . . power   *between giving judgement and carrying it out*

[173] potency . . . good   *power being asserted (in this following decree)*

[178] trunk   *body*

[181] sith   *since*

Nor are those empty-hearted whose low sounds
Reverb no hollowness.

LEAR   Kent, on thy life, no more!

KENT My life I never held but as a pawn
To wage against thine enemies; nor fear to lose it,
Thy safety being motive.

LEAR   Out of my sight!

KENT See better, Lear, and let me still remain
The true blank of thine eye.   160

LEAR Now by Apollo –

KENT   Now by Apollo, king,
Thou swear'st thy gods in vain.

LEAR   O vassal! miscreant!

He reaches for his sword acts on emotion without thought

ALBANY, CORNWALL Dear sir, forbear!

KENT Kill thy physician, and thy fee bestow kill the one
Upon the foul disease. Revoke thy gift, supporting you
Or whilst I can vent clamour from my throat and aid
I'll tell thee thou dost evil. the ones

LEAR   Hear me, recreant, against you
On thine allegiance, hear me!
That thou hast sought to make us break our vow,
Which we durst never yet, and with strained pride   170
To come betwixt our sentence and our power,
Which nor our nature nor our place can bear,
Our potency made good, take thy reward.
Five days we do allot thee for provision
To shield thee from disasters of the world,
And on the sixth to turn thy hated back
Upon our kingdom. If on the tenth day following
Thy banished trunk be found in our dominions,
The moment is thy death. Away! By Jupiter,
This shall not be revoked.   180

KENT Fare thee well, king; sith thus thou wilt
     appear,
Freedom lives hence and banishment is here.

Freedom can't be found in kingdom
w/ king such as Lear

39

[185] your . . . approve *may your deeds prove your grand speeches true*

[186] effects *practical results*

[188] shape . . . course *conduct himself as before*

[192] in the least *at the lowest*

[193] present *immediate*

[197] so *dear in value*

[199] little . . . substance *object which seems small (in comparison with one-third of England)*

[200] pieced *joined on to it*

[201] fitly like *suitably appeal to*

[203] owes *owns*

[205] strangered *made a stranger*

[207] Election . . . up *it is impossible to choose her*

[*To* CORDELIA] The gods to their dear shelter take
thee, maid,
That justly think'st and hast most rightly said.
[*To* GONERIL *and* REGAN] And your large speeches
may your deeds approve,
That good effects may spring from words of love.
Thus Kent, O princes, bids you all adieu;
He'll shape his old course in a country new. [*Exit*

Flourish. Enter GLOUCESTER, *with* FRANCE,
BURGUNDY *and* ATTENDANTS

GLOUCESTER Here's France and Burgundy, my noble
lord.
LEAR My lord of Burgundy,   190
We first address toward you, who with this king
Hath rivalled for our daughter. What in the least
Will you require in present dower with her,
Or cease your quest of love?
BURGUNDY   Most royal majesty,
I crave no more than hath your highness offered,
Nor will you tender less.
LEAR   Right noble Burgundy,
When she was dear to us, we did hold her so,
But now her price is fallen. Sir, there she stands.
If aught within that little seeming substance,
Or all of it, with our displeasure pieced,   200
And nothing more, may fitly like your grace,
She's there, and she is yours.
BURGUNDY   I know no answer.
LEAR Will you, with those infirmities she owes,
Unfriended, new adopted to our hate,
Dowered with our curse and strangered with our
oath,
Take her or leave her?
BURGUNDY   Pardon me, royal sir,
Election makes not up in such conditions.
LEAR Then leave her, sir, for by the power that made me

[210] make . . . stray *wander so far*

[212] T'avert your liking *to turn your love*
        more worthier *This 'double' form of the comparative was*
quite common.

[215] your best object *object of your greatest love*

[216] argument *theme*
[217] trice *brief moment*
[218] dismantle *strip away*

[221] That monsters it *as to be monstrous*
[221–22] or . . . taint *or else your previously granted affection*
becomes suspect
[223–4] Must . . . in me *demands a faith which can't be*
achieved by reason alone, but needs miracles

[225] If for *if the trouble is that*
[226] and purpose not *without meaning to put what I say into*
practice

[232] still-soliciting *always looking for benefit*

[234] lost *ruined*

[236] tardiness in nature *natural reticence*
[237–8] leaves . . . That *gives no spoken account of what*

I tell you all her wealth. [*To* FRANCE] For you,
    great king,
I would not from your love make such a stray   210
To match you where I hate; therefore beseech you
T'avert your liking a more worthier way
Than on a wretch whom Nature is ashamed
Almost t' acknowledge hers.

FRANCE   This is most strange,
That she whom even but now was your best
    object,
The argument of your praise, balm of your age,
The best, the dearest, should in this trice of time
Commit a thing so monstrous to dismantle
So many folds of favour. Sure her offence
Must be of such unnatural degree   220
That monsters it, or your fore-vouched affection
Fall into taint; which to believe of her
Must be a faith that reason without miracle
Should never plant in me.

CORDELIA   I yet beseech your majesty –
If for I want that glib and oily art
To speak and purpose not, since what I well
    intend,
I'll do 't before I speak – that you make known
It is no vicious blot, murder or foulness,
No unchaste action or dishonoured step,
That hath deprived me of your grace and favour;   230
But even for want of that for which I am richer,
A still-soliciting eye, and such a tongue
That I am glad I have not, though not to have it
Hath lost me in your liking.

LEAR   Better thou
Hadst not been born than not t' have pleased me
    better.

FRANCE Is it but this – a tardiness in nature
Which often leaves the history unspoke
That it intends to do? My lord of Burgundy,

43

[240] regards *considerations*
     stands *The plural form in -s was not uncommon.*
[241] Aloof . . . point *remote from the essential issue*

[243] portion *dowry*

[250] respects of fortune *considerations of wealth*

[257] inflamed respect *most warm regard*
[258] to my chance *as a piece of good fortune to me*

[260] waterish Burgundy *that well-watered country with its well-watered wine*
[262] unkind *lacking in natural affection*
[263] Thou . . . find *by losing this place, you find a better* ('*here*' *and* '*where*' *treated as nouns*)

[267] benison *blessing*

ACT ONE, SCENE ONE

What say you to the lady? Love's not love
When it is mingled with regards that stands   240
Aloof from th' entire point. Will you have her?
She is herself a dowry.

BURGUNDY   Royal king,
Give but that portion which yourself proposed,
And here I take Cordelia by the hand,
Duchess of Burgundy.

LEAR Nothing. I have sworn; I am firm.

BURGUNDY I am sorry then you have so lost a father
That you must lose a husband.

CORDELIA Peace be with Burgundy!
Since that respects of fortune are his love,   250
I shall not be his wife.

FRANCE Fairest Cordelia, that art most rich, being
    poor,
Most choice, forsaken, and most loved, despised,
Thee and thy virtues here I seize upon;
Be it lawful I take up what's cast away.
Gods, gods! 'Tis strange that from their cold'st
    neglect
My love should kindle to inflamed respect.
Thy dowerless daughter, king, thrown to my
    chance,
Is queen of us, of ours, and our fair France.
Not all the dukes of waterish Burgundy   260
Can buy this unprized precious maid of me.
Bid them farewell, Cordelia, though unkind;
Thou losest here, a better where to find.

LEAR Thou hast her, France; let her be thine, for we
Have no such daughter, nor shall ever see
That face of hers again. Therefore be gone
Without our grace, our love, our benison.
Come, noble Burgundy.

> [*Flourish. Exeunt* LEAR, BURGUNDY,
> CORNWALL, ALBANY *and* ATTENDANTS

France is impressed by what she says and is

[269] washed eyes   *They are wet with tears, but they are washed clean of all illusion.*

[272] as ... named   *by their proper names*

[273] professéd bosoms   *the love you have professed*

[275] prefer   *promote*

[279] At Fortune's alms   *at Fortune's alms-giving, hence 'as something given away by Fortune'*
　　　scanted   *been deficient in*
[280] worth ... wanted   *deserve the denial of that affection which you have shown yourself to lack*
[281] plighted   *pleated, concealed in folds*
[282] covert ... derides   *in the end exposes to shame and derision*

[286] will hence   *will leave here*

[297] look   *expect*

FRANCE   Bid farewell to your sisters.

CORDELIA The jewels of our father, with washed
    eyes   270
    Cordelia leaves you. I know you what you are,
    And like a sister am most loath to call
    Your faults as they are named. Love well our
        father.
    To your professéd bosoms I commit him,
    But yet, alas, stood I within his grace,
    I would prefer him to a better place.
    So farewell to you both.

REGAN Prescribe not us our duty.

GONERIL   Let your study
    Be to content your lord, who hath received you
    At Fortune's alms. You have obedience scanted,
    And well are worth the want that you have   280
        wanted.

CORDELIA Time shall unfold what plighted cunning
        hides,
    Who covert faults at last with shame derides.
    Well may you prosper.

FRANCE   Come, my fair Cordelia.
                    [*Exeunt* FRANCE *and* CORDELIA

GONERIL Sister, it is not little I have to say of what
    most nearly appertains to us both. I think our father
    will hence tonight.

REGAN That's most certain, and with you; next
    month with us.

GONERIL You see how full of changes his age is. The
    observation we have made of it hath not been little. 290
    He always loved our sister most, and with what poor
    judgement he hath now cast her off appears too
    grossly.

REGAN 'Tis the infirmity of his age; yet he hath ever
    but slenderly known himself.

GONERIL The best and soundest of his time hath been
    but rash; then must we look from his age to receive,

[298] **long-engraffed** *firmly implanted (engrafted)*

[299] **waywardness** *contrariness*

[301] **unconstant starts** *sudden impulses*

[303] **compliment** *ceremony*

[304-5] **hit together** *act in concert*

[305] **carry authority** *continues to use his authority*

[305-6] **disposition** *temperament*

[306] **last surrender** *giving away the kingdom*

[309] **i' th' heat** *while the iron is hot*

ACT ONE, scene 2

Lear's angry and hasty disruption of his family, which initiates the main plot, is followed in this scene by Edmund's cool and premeditated disruption of his family in the parallel sub-plot. Age and youth are again strongly contrasted.

[1-2] **Thou . . . bound** *After Lear's appeal to gods who govern men's lives, Edmund acknowledges only nature and her law. He does not mean 'natural law' as anciently understood, by which all nature obeyed a divine order, but the more modern 'law of nature', by which we are to follow the promptings of our desires (in the present case, the desire to assert oneself over others).*

[3] **Stand . . . custom** *submit to unhealthy convention*

[4] **curiosity of nations** *over-meticulousness of civilised law*

[5] **moonshines** *months*

[6] **Lag of** *behind (in time). Edmund loses his inheritance because he is younger, as well as illegitimate.*

  base *a technical term for illegitimate children*

[7] **compact** *knit together*

[9] **honest** *virtuous*

[11] **lusty . . . nature** *vigorous theft of natural pleasure*

[11-12] **take . . . quality** *require (for their conception) better personal qualities and ardour (in the parents)*

[19] **speed** *is successful*

[20] **invention** *scheme*

not alone the imperfections of long-engraffed condition, but therewithal the unruly waywardness that
infirm and choleric years bring with them.   300

REGAN Such unconstant starts are we like to have from
him as this of Kent's banishment.

GONERIL There is further compliment of leave-taking
between France and him. Pray you let us hit together. If our father carry authority with such disposition as he bears, this last surrender of his will but
offend us.

REGAN We shall further think of it.

GONERIL We must do something, and i' th' heat.

[*Exeunt*

Scene 2. *Enter* EDMUND

EDMUND Thou, Nature, art my goddess; to thy law
My services are bound. Wherefore should I
Stand in the plague of custom, and permit
The curiosity of nations to deprive me,
For that I am some twelve or fourteen moonshines
Lag of a brother? Why bastard? wherefore base?
When my dimensions are as well compact,
My mind as generous, and my shape as true,
As honest madam's issue? Why brand they us
With base? with baseness? bastardy? base, base?   10
Who in the lusty stealth of nature take
More composition and fierce quality
Than doth, within a dull, stale, tired bed,
Go to th' creating a whole tribe of fops
Got 'tween a sleep and wake? Well then,
Legitimate Edgar, I must have your land.
Our father's love is to the bastard Edmund
As to th' legitimate. Fine word, 'legitimate'!
Well, my legitimate, if this letter speed,
And my invention thrive, Edmund the base   20

[21] top *overcome*

[23] in choler parted *departed in anger. This is not witnessed on stage.*
[24] Prescribed *limited*
[25] exhibition *an allowance of money*
[26] Upon the gad *impulsively*

[28] put up *put away*

[34] dispatch *hasty conveying*

[39] for so much as *on the evidence of that part which*
[40] o'erlooking *inspection*

[43] to blame *blameworthy*

[46] essay *trial*
[47] policy and reverence *self-interested strategy of reverence*
[48] best . . . times *prime of our life*
[49] oldness *senility*
[50] fond *foolish*
[51] sways *rules*
[52] suffered *allowed (by youth)*

Shall top th' legitimate. I grow, I prosper.
Now, gods, stand up for bastards!

Enter GLOUCESTER

GLOUCESTER Kent banished thus? and France in
    choler parted?
And the king gone tonight? Prescribed his power?
Confined to exhibition? All this done
Upon the gad? – Edmund, how now? What news?
EDMUND So please your lordship, none.

                    [*Hiding the letter*

GLOUCESTER Why so earnestly seek you to put up that
    letter?
EDMUND I know no news, my lord.   30
GLOUCESTER What paper were you reading?
EDMUND Nothing, my lord.
GLOUCESTER No? What needed then that terrible
    dispatch of it into your pocket? The quality of
    nothing hath not such need to hide itself. Let's see.
    Come, if it be nothing, I shall not need spectacles.
EDMUND I beseech you, sir, pardon me. It is a letter
    from my brother that I have not all o'er-read; and
    for so much as I have perused, I find it not fit for
    your o'erlooking.   40
GLOUCESTER Give me the letter, sir.
EDMUND I shall offend either to detain or give it. The
    contents, as in part I understand them, are to blame.
GLOUCESTER Let's see, let's see.
EDMUND I hope, for my brother's justification, he
    wrote this but as an essay or taste of my virtue.
GLOUCESTER [*Reads*] *This policy and reverence of age*
    makes the world bitter to the best of our times, keeps
    our fortunes from us till our oldness cannot relish them.
    I begin to find an idle and fond bondage in the oppres-   50
    sion of aged tyranny, who sways, not as it hath power,
    but as it is suffered. Come to me, that of this I may

51

[53] till I waked him *which would be never*

[62] closet *room*
[63] character *handwriting*

[66] in . . . that *seeing what in fact it is*
[67] fain *gladly*

[71] sounded you *tried you out*

[74] perfect *mature*

[78] detested *detestable*

[85] certain *correct and safe*

[89] pawn down *wager*

speak more. If our father would sleep till I waked him,
you should enjoy half his revenue for ever, and live the
beloved of your brother. Edgar.

Hum! Conspiracy! 'Sleep till I waked him, you
should enjoy half his revenue.' My son Edgar! Had
he a hand to write this? A heart and brain to breed
it in? When came you to this? Who brought it?

EDMUND It was not brought me, my lord; there's the 60
cunning of it. I found it thrown in at the casement of
my closet.

GLOUCESTER You know the character to be your
brother's?

EDMUND If the matter were good, my lord, I durst
swear it were his; but, in respect of that, I would
fain think it were not.

GLOUCESTER It is his.

EDMUND It is his hand, my lord; but I hope his heart
is not in the contents.   70

GLOUCESTER Has he never before sounded you in this
business?

EDMUND Never, my lord. But I have heard him oft
maintain it to be fit that, sons at perfect age, and
fathers declined, the father should be as ward to the
son, and the son manage his revenue.

GLOUCESTER O villain, villain! His very opinion in the
letter! Abhorred villain! Unnatural, detested,
brutish villain! Worse than brutish! Go, sirrah, seek
him. I'll apprehend him. Abominable villain! 80
Where is he?

EDMUND I do not well know, my lord. If it shall
please you to suspend your indignation against my
brother till you can derive from him better testi-
mony of his intent, you should run a certain course;
where, if you violently proceed against him, mis-
taking his purpose, it would make a great gap in your
own honour, and shake in pieces the heart of his
obedience. I dare pawn down my life for him that he

[90] feel *test*
[91] pretence of danger *dangerous intention*

[95] auricular assurance *proof offered by your own ears*

[101] wind . . . him *work your way into his thoughts*
[102–3] unstate myself *forfeit my earldom*
[103] in . . . resolution *fully free from doubt*
[104] presently *immediately*
      convey *carry forward*

[107] late *recent*
[108–10] Though . . . effects *though science can explain why
eclipses happen we still suffer from the disasters which follow them*
[108] wisdom of nature *natural science*

[114] comes . . . prediction *falls within what is predicted for us*
[115] falls . . . nature *ceases to show natural affection*
[116–7] We . . . time *Gloucester's speech as a whole is a
classic representation of the feelings of every generation as old age
draws near.*
[117] hollowness *insincerity*
[118] disquietly *disturbingly*
[119–20] it . . . nothing *you will gain by it*

[123] foppery *folly*
[124–5] sick . . . behaviour *down in the world, often through our
own fault (a medical metaphor)*

hath writ this to feel my affection to your honour, 90
and to no other pretence of danger.

GLOUCESTER Think you so?

EDMUND If your honour judge it meet, I will place
you where you shall hear us confer of this and by an
auricular assurance have your satisfaction, and that
without any further delay than this very evening.

GLOUCESTER He cannot be such a monster!

EDMUND Nor is not, sure.

GLOUCESTER To his father, that so tenderly and entirely loves him! Heaven and earth! Edmund, seek 100
him out; wind me into him, I pray you; frame the
business after your own wisdom. I would unstate
myself to be in a due resolution.

EDMUND I will seek him, sir, presently, convey the
business as I shall find means, and acquaint you
withal.

GLOUCESTER These late eclipses in the sun and moon
portend no good to us. Though the wisdom of nature
can reason it thus and thus, yet nature finds itself
scourged by the sequent effects. Love cools, friend- 110
ship falls off, brothers divide. In cities, mutinies; in
countries, discord; in palaces, treason; and the
bond cracked 'twixt son and father. This villain of
mine comes under the prediction; there's son against
father: the king falls from bias of nature; there's
father against child. We have seen the best of our
time. Machinations, hollowness, treachery, and all
ruinous disorders follow us disquietly to our graves.
Find out this villain, Edmund; it shall lose thee
nothing; do it carefully. And the noble and true- 120
hearted Kent banished; his offence, honesty! 'Tis
strange.   [*Exit*

EDMUND This is the excellent foppery of the world
that when we are sick in fortune, often the surfeits of
our own behaviour, we make guilty of our disasters
the sun, the moon and stars; as if we were villains

Gloucester blames all on fate and nature causing (handwritten margin note)

[128] treachers *traitors*

    by . . . predominance *by a planet being in a superior position*

[131] divine . . . on *supernatural enforcement*

[132] whoremaster *lecherous*

[132-3] lay . . . star *hold a star responsible for his lustfulness*

[133-4] compounded *came together. This intercourse, which shapes Gloucester's fate, is mentioned four times, I. 1. 12-23, here, IV. 6. 114-16, and V. 3. 171.*

[134] Dragon's tail *a particular configuration of sun and moon*

[135] Ursa Major *the Great Bear*

[136] Fut *explosive sound of disgust*

[138] bastardising *being conceived out of wedlock*

[139] Pat *just at the right time*

    like . . . comedy *as predictably as the routine endings of old plays*

[141] Tom o'Bedlam *name given to the mad beggars whom Edgar later imitates. Bedlam is short for Bethlehem, the name of the madhouse in North London.*

[142] Fa . . . mi *He sighs out a musical phrase.*

[149] succeed *follow*

[151-2] maledictions *curses*

[152-3] diffidences *failures of trust*

[153-4] dissipation of cohorts *scattering of armies*

[155-6] *sectary astronomical* believer in the stars

ACT ONE, SCENE TWO

on necessity, fools by heavenly compulsion, knaves,
thieves, and treachers by spherical predominance,
drunkards, liars, and adulterers by an enforced
obedience of planetary influence, and all that we are 130
evil in by a divine thrusting on. An admirable
evasion of whoremaster man, to lay his goatish disposition to the charge of a star! My father compounded with my mother under the Dragon's tail,
and my nativity was under Ursa Major, so that it
follows I am rough and lecherous. Fut, I should
have been that I am, had the maidenliest star in the
firmament twinkled on my bastardising. Edgar –

Enter EDGAR

Pat he comes, like the catastrophe of the old comedy.
My cue is villainous melancholy, with a sigh like 140
Tom o' Bedlam – O these eclipses do portend these
divisions. Fa, sol, la, mi.

EDGAR How now, brother Edmund? What serious
contemplation are you in?

EDMUND I am thinking, brother, of a prediction I read
this other day, what should follow these eclipses.

EDGAR Do you busy yourself with that?

EDMUND I promise you, the effects he writes of
succeed unhappily, as of unnaturalness between the
child and the parent, death, dearth, dissolutions of 150
ancient amities, divisions in state, menaces and maledictions against king and nobles, needless diffidences, banishment of friends, dissipation of
cohorts, nuptial breaches, and I know not what.

EDGAR How long have you been a sectary astronomical?

EDMUND When saw you my father last?

EDGAR The night gone by.

EDMUND Spake you with him?

EDGAR Ay, two hours together.   160

[166] qualified *lessened*

[168] mischief . . . person *injury to you*
[169] allay *diminish*

[171–2] continent forbearance *patient restraint*

[174] fitly *at a suitable occasion*

[180–81] but faintly *only in outline*

[188] practices *plots*
[190] All . . . fit *anything is proper that I can turn to my convenience*

ACT ONE, scene 3

In the Duke of Albany's palace, Goneril begins to put into practice the ideas about governing the old which we have heard about in the last scene. Lear is obviously a difficult parent. Is Goneril an evil woman or an exasperated daughter in this brief scene?

EDMUND Parted you in good terms? Found you no
displeasure in him, by word nor countenance?

EDGAR None at all.

EDMUND Bethink yourself wherein you may have
offended him; and at my entreaty forbear his
presence until some little time hath qualified the
heat of his displeasure, which at this instant so
rageth in him that with the mischief of your person
it would scarcely allay.

EDGAR Some villain hath done me wrong.   170

EDMUND That's my fear. I pray you have a continent
forbearance till the speed of his rage goes slower;
and, as I say, retire with me to my lodging, from
whence I will fitly bring you to hear my lord speak.
Pray ye, go; there's my key. If you do stir abroad,
go armed.

EDGAR Armed, brother?

EDMUND Brother, I advise you to the best. I am no
honest man if there be any good meaning toward
you. I have told you what I have seen and heard but 180
faintly, nothing like the image and horror of it.
Pray you, away!

EDGAR Shall I hear from you anon?

EDMUND I do serve you in this business.

[*Exit* EDGAR

A credulous father! and a brother noble
Whose nature is so far from doing harms
That he suspects none; on whose foolish honesty
My practices ride easy! I see the business.
Let me, if not by birth, have lands by wit;
All with me's meet that I can fashion fit.   [*Exit* 190

Scene 3. *Enter* GONERIL *and* OSWALD, *her steward*

GONERIL Did my father strike my gentleman for chid-
ing of his fool?

[7] knights *the hundred knights which Lear insisted should follow him, to be maintained by his daughters*

[10] come . . . services *reduce the level of service*

[14] have . . . question *make an issue of it*

[15] distaste *dislike*

[17] Idle *foolish*

[21] With checks . . . abused *with rebukes as well as flattery, when flattery is seen to have bad results. She thinks Lear is behaving the worse because she and Regan have flattered him so much.*

[25] breed . . . occasions *bring about favourable opportunities*

[26] straight *at once*

[27] to hold . . . course *to take exactly the same course as I am doing*

ACT ONE, scene 4

In this scene Lear begins to understand what he has done, to himself and to Cordelia. There is continuous insistence from the Fool that Lear has committed the absurdity of abolishing himself. Once again, Lear takes refuge in titanic wrath and denunciation of a daughter.

[1] as well *as successfully (as he has disguised himself)*

[2] diffuse *change to another form*

OSWALD Ay, madam.

GONERIL By day and night he wrongs me. Every
  hour
  He flashes into one gross crime or other
  That sets us all at odds. I'll not endure it.
  His knights grow riotous, and himself upbraids us
  On every trifle. When he returns from hunting
  I will not speak with him. Say I am sick.
  If you come slack of former services,   10
  You shall do well; the fault of it I'll answer.

OSWALD He's coming, madam; I hear him.

GONERIL Put on what weary negligence you please,
  You and your fellows; I'd have it come to
    question.
  If he distaste it, let him to my sister,
  Whose mind and mine I know in that are one,
  Not to be overruled. Idle old man,
  That still would manage those authorities
  That he hath given away! Now, by my life,
  Old fools are babes again, and must be used   20
  With checks as flatteries, when they are seen
    abused.
  Remember what I have said.

OSWALD   Well, madam.

GONERIL And let his knights have colder looks
    among you;
  What grows of it, no matter. Advise your fellows
    so.
  I would breed from hence occasions, and I shall,
  That I may speak. I'll write straight to my sister
  To hold my very course. Prepare for dinner.
                                          [*Exeunt*

Scene 4. *Enter* KENT, *disguised*

KENT If but as well I other accents borrow,
  That can my speech diffuse, my good intent

[3] that full issue   *the reconciliation of Lear and Cordelia. See Introduction pages* 18–19.

[4] razed my likeness   *blotted out my usual appearance*
[Horns]   *the sound of hunting horns*
[within]   *off-stage*

[8] stay   *wait*

[12] What . . . profess?   *what is your occupation?*

[14] profess   *claim*

[17] judgement   *the eternal judgement of the soul*

[31] Authority   *Kent is not flattering, though Lear is flattered. Kent, who freely chooses the conditions of feudal service, acknowledges only the king as the source of authority. It is his duty to help his master to re-assert the authority which he has squandered.*

[33] honest counsel   *honourable secrets*

May carry through itself to that full issue
For which I razed my likeness. Now, banished
    Kent,
If thou canst serve where thou dost stand
    condemned,
So may it come thy master whom thou lov'st
Shall find thee full of labours.   *[Horns within*

Enter LEAR, KNIGHTS *and* ATTENDANTS

LEAR Let me not stay a jot for dinner; go get it
ready.

    [Exit ATTENDANT

How now! what art thou?   10

KENT A man, sir.

LEAR What dost thou profess? What wouldst thou
with us?

KENT I do profess to be no less than I seem, to serve
him truly that will put me in trust, to love him that
is honest, to converse with him that is wise and says
little, to fear judgement, to fight when I cannot
choose, and to eat no fish.

LEAR What art thou?

KENT A very honest-hearted fellow, and as poor as   20
the king.

LEAR If thou be'st as poor for a subject as he's for a
king, thou art poor enough. What wouldst thou?

KENT Service.

LEAR Who wouldst thou serve?

KENT You.

LEAR Dost thou know me, fellow?

KENT No, sir; but you have that in your countenance
which I would fain call master.

LEAR What's that?   30

KENT Authority.

LEAR What services canst thou do?

KENT I can keep honest counsel, ride, run, mar a

[34] curious   *elaborate (not plain and straightforward)*

[43] knave   *boy*
     fool   *jester*

[47] clotpoll   *blockhead*

[58–9] entertained   *treated*

[61] general dependants   *servants generally*

curious tale in telling it, and deliver a plain message
bluntly. That which ordinary men are fit for I am
qualified in, and the best of me is diligence.

LEAR How old art thou?

KENT Not so young, sir, to love a woman for singing,
nor so old to dote on her for anything. I have years
on my back forty-eight.   40

LEAR Follow me; thou shalt serve me. If I like thee
no worse after dinner I will not part from thee yet.
Dinner, ho! dinner! Where's my knave? my fool?
Go you and call my fool hither.

         [*Exit another* ATTENDANT

Enter OSWALD

You! you, sirrah! Where's my daughter?

OSWALD So please you—   [*Exit*

LEAR What says the fellow there? Call the clotpoll
back!

            [*Exit* KNIGHT

Where's my fool? Ho! I think the world's asleep.

Enter KNIGHT

How now? Where's that mongrel?   50

KNIGHT He says, my lord, your daughter is not well.

LEAR Why came not the slave back to me when I
called him?

KNIGHT Sir, he answered me in the roundest manner
he would not.

LEAR He would not?

KNIGHT My lord, I know not what the matter is,
but to my judgement your highness is not entertained with that ceremonious affection as you were
wont. There's a great abatement of kindness appears   60
as well in the general dependants as in the duke
himself also and your daughter.

[67] rememberest *reminds*
[67–8] conception *notion*
[69–70] jealous curiosity *suspicious attention to detail*
[70] very pretence *real intention*

[74] fool . . . away *The grief which the Fool suffers over the banishment of Cordelia gives his jesting a special edge of pathos.*

[84] bandy *exchange; hit back (as in tennis)*

[86] football *(at that time, a low-class street game)*

[89] differences *i.e. between social positions*
[90] lubber *clumsy oaf*
[91] Go to *come along now!*
[91–2] have you wisdom? *do you know what's good for you?*

LEAR Ha! say'st thou so?

KNIGHT I beseech you pardon me, my lord, if I be mistaken, for my duty cannot be silent when I think your highness wronged.

LEAR Thou but rememberest me of mine own conception. I have perceived a most faint neglect of late, which I have rather blamed as mine own jealous curiosity than as a very pretence and purpose of un- 70 kindness. I will look further into't. But where's my fool? I have not seen him this two days.

KNIGHT Since my young lady's going into France, sir, the fool hath much pined away.

LEAR No more of that; I have noted it well. Go you and tell my daughter I would speak with her.

[Exit an ATTENDANT

Go you, call hither my fool.

[Exit another ATTENDANT

Enter OSWALD

O you sir, you, come you hither, sir. Who am I, sir?

OSWALD My lady's father.

LEAR My lady's father? My lord's knave! You 80 whoreson dog, you slave, you cur!

OSWALD I am none of these, my lord, I beseech your pardon.

LEAR Do you bandy looks with me, you rascal?

[Strikes him

OSWALD I'll not be strucken, my lord.

KENT Nor tripped neither, you base football player.

[Tripping up his heels

LEAR I thank thee, fellow. Thou serv'st me, and I'll love thee.

KENT Come, sir, arise, away! I'll teach you differences. Away, away! If you will measure your lubber's 90 length again, tarry; but away! Go to; have you wisdom? So. *[Exit* OSWALD

[94] earnest of   *some money in advance for*

[95] coxcomb   *fool's cap*

[100] an   *if*
   smile . . . sits   *enjoy the favourable wind*

[102–3] banished . . . will   *An expression of love from as per-verse a person as Lear is a punishment: to be away from his mis-guided acts is a blessing.*

[104–10] How now . . . thy daughters   *The Fool has pointedly ignored Lear; he now turns to him, wishing he had another fool's cap for him to wear. Lear has given away everything, even the know-ledge of his own folly. The Fool can give him some indication of his folly (one coxcomb); the rest of Lear's self-knowledge he will have to obtain via the actions of his daughters.*

[105] nuncle   *familiar form of 'uncle'*

[113] the lady brach   *that refined bitch, untruth*

[115] gall   *bitterness. Lear may be thinking of the Fool, Oswald, or his own deeds.*

[119–28] *This riddling rhyme mockingly advocates prudential caution and reserve as a means of building up possessions: the oppo-site extreme of Lear's impulsive rashness.*

[121] owest   *own*

[123] trowest   *believe in*

[124] Set . . . throwest   *keep money in reserve when you gamble (?)*

LEAR Now, my friendly knave, I thank thee. There's earnest of thy service.

Enter FOOL

FOOL Let me hire him too. Here's my coxcomb.

LEAR How now, my pretty knave? How dost thou?

FOOL Sirrah, you were best take my coxcomb.

KENT Why, fool?

FOOL Why? For taking one's part that's out of favour. Nay, an thou canst not smile as the wind sits, thou'lt 100 catch cold shortly. There, take my coxcomb! Why, this fellow has banished two on's daughters, and did the third a blessing against his will. If thou follow him thou must needs wear my coxcomb. How now, nuncle? Would I had two coxcombs and two daughters!

LEAR Why, my boy?

FOOL If I gave them all my living, I'd keep my coxcombs myself. There's mine; beg another of thy daughters. 110

LEAR Take heed, sirrah – the whip.

FOOL Truth's a dog must to kennel; he must be whipped out, when the lady brach may stand by th' fire and stink.

LEAR A pestilent gall to me!

FOOL Sirrah, I'll teach thee a speech.

LEAR Do.

FOOL Mark it, nuncle!

> Have more than thou showest,
> Speak less than thou knowest, 120
> Lend less than thou owest,
> Ride more than thou goest,
> Learn more than thou trowest,
> Set less than thou throwest;
> Leave thy drink and thy whore,
> And keep in-a-door,

the Fool reveals Leer's faults to him

[130] unfeed   *unpaid*

[133-4] nothing . . . nothing   *See I. 1. 91*

[141] That lord   *Lear himself*

[147] motley   *a coloured tweed worn by fools*

[150] All . . . away   *contradicting Lear's view that he could keep his titles when he gave away his power (I. 1. 137)*

[152] not . . . fool   *not entirely a fool. But the Fool pretends to understand him to mean 'not the whole world of fools'.*

[154] had . . . out   *had been granted a monopoly (as courtiers notoriously were for all sorts of activities and manufactures at this time)*

[161] clovest   *split*
[162-3] bor'st . . . dirt   *This occurs, as a sign of extreme stupidity, in numerous folk tales.*

And thou shalt have more
Than two tens to a score.

KENT This is nothing, fool.

FOOL Then 'tis like the breath of an unfeed lawyer – 130
you gave me nothing for't. Can you make no use of
nothing, nuncle?

LEAR Why, no, boy; nothing can be made out of
nothing.

FOOL [*To* KENT] Prithee tell him, so much the rent of
his land comes to. He will not believe a fool.

LEAR A bitter fool!

FOOL Dost thou know the difference, my boy, between a bitter fool and a sweet one?

LEAR No, lad; teach me. 140

FOOL   That lord that counselled thee
      To give away thy land,
    Come place him here by me –
      Do thou for him stand.
    The sweet and bitter fool
      Will presently appear:
    The one in motley here,
      The other found out – there!

LEAR Dost thou call me fool, boy?

FOOL All thy other titles thou hast given away; that 150
thou wast born with.

KENT This is not altogether fool, my lord.

FOOL No, faith, lords and great men will not let me.
If I had a monopoly out, they would have part on't;
and ladies too, they will not let me have all the fool to
myself; they'll be snatching. Nuncle, give me an egg,
and I'll give thee two crowns.

LEAR What two crowns shall they be?

FOOL Why, after I have cut the egg i'th' middle and
eat up the meat, the two crowns of the egg. When 160
thou clovest thy crown i'th' middle and gav'st away
both parts, thou bor'st thine ass on thy back o'er the
dirt. Thou hadst little wit in thy bald crown when

[167] grace *favour*

[168] foppish *foolish*

[169–70] And . . . apish *fools don't know how to show their talents since wise men ape them so in their behaviour*

[171] When . . . wont *how long have you been accustomed*

[177] play bo-peep *hide himself (infant's game)*

[182] I . . . kin *I am curious to know what relationship*

[190–91] What . . . on? *What are you doing with that headband on?*

[193–4] O . . . figure *This repeats the Fool's basic point. If the number 10 loses just a part of itself, the figure 1, it becomes nothing: so Lear has destroyed himself by losing a part of himself.*

thou gav'st thy golden one away. If I speak like
myself in this, let him be whipped that first finds it
so.

    [*Sings*]   Fools had ne'er less grace in a year;
                For wise men are grown foppish,
                And know not how their wits to wear,
                Their manners are so apish.   170

LEAR When were you wont to be so full of songs, sirrah?

FOOL I have used it, nuncle, e'er since thou mad'st thy
daughters thy mothers; for when thou gav'st them
the rod and putt'st down thine own breeches,

    [*Sings*]   Then they for sudden joy did weep,
                And I for sorrow sung,
                That such a king should play bo-peep,
                And go the fools among.

Prithee, nuncle, keep a schoolmaster that can teach
thy fool to lie; I would fain learn to lie.   180

LEAR An you lie, sirrah, we'll have you whipped.

FOOL I marvel what kin thou and thy daughters are;
they'll have me whipped for speaking true, thou'lt
have me whipped for lying; and sometimes I am
whipped for holding my peace. I had rather be any
kind o' thing than a fool; and yet I would not be
thee, nuncle. Thou hast pared thy wit o' both sides
and left nothing i'th' middle. Here comes one o' the
parings.

Enter GONERIL

LEAR How now, daughter? What makes that front- 190
let on? You are too much of late i'th' frown.

FOOL Thou wast a pretty fellow when thou hadst no
need to care for her frowning; now thou art an O
without a figure. I am better than thou art now; I
am a fool, thou art nothing. [*To* GONERIL] Yes,
forsooth, I will hold my tongue; so your face bids
me, though you say nothing.

[201] shelled peascod   *a pod empty of peas*
[202] all-licensed   *permitted to do anything*

[205] rank   *gross*

[208] too late   *all too recently*
[209] put it on   *forward it*

[212] in . . . weal   *in solicitude for a healthy community*

[214–5] Which . . . proceeding   *which in other circumstances would be shameful for you but in view of their necessity will be seen as wise measures*

[218] it head . . . it young   *its (baby language)*
[219] darkling   *in the dark*
[220–37] *Lear now begins some exaggerated play-acting—a mock-serious enquiry who Goneril and Regan may be. There is deep irony in his comic turn, for to rediscover who he and his children are becomes his most serious need.*
[222] fraught   *stored*

[225] May . . . know   *may not even a donkey like me know*

[226] Whoop . . . thee   *probably a refrain from an old song. 'Jug' can be either a woman's nickname, or the bottle.*

[229] notion   *mental capacity*

Mum, mum:
He that keeps nor crust nor crumb,
Weary of all, shall want some.   200

[*Pointing to* LEAR] That's a shelled peascod.

GONERIL Not only, sir, this your all-licensed fool,
But other of your insolent retinue
Do hourly carp and quarrel, breaking forth
In rank and not-to-be-endured riots. Sir,
I had thought, by making this well known unto
   you,
To have found a safe redress; but now grow
   fearful,
By what yourself too late have spoke and done,
That you protect this course, and put it on
By your allowance; which if you should, the fault   210
Would not scape censure, nor the redress sleep
Which in the tender of a wholesome weal
Might in their working do you that offence
Which else were shame, that then necessity
Will call discreet proceeding.

FOOL For you know, nuncle,
   The hedge-sparrow fed the cuckoo so long
   That it's had it head bit off by it young.
So out went the candle, and we were left darkling.

LEAR Are you our daughter?   220

GONERIL I would you would make use of your good
   wisdom
(Whereof I know you are fraught) and put away
These dispositions which of late transport you
From what you rightly are.

FOOL May not an ass know when the cart draws the
   horse?
               Whoop, Jug! I love thee.

LEAR Does any here know me? This is not Lear.
Does Lear walk thus, speak thus? Where are his
   eyes?
Either his notion weakens, his discernings

[margin, handwritten:] Formal speech makes her appear more in the right against his unorthodox manner

[margin, handwritten:] How can people act like this? Is he not the Right

75

[230] lethargied *drugged*

[233] that *who I am*
[233-5] by . . . daughters *if I were to go by my kingship, my knowledge, and reason, I should come to the mistaken conclusion that I had daughters*
[236] Which . . . make *and they will make him*

[238] admiration *wonderment*
     o' th' savour *the same taste*

[243-7] *How far is Goneril's charge true? Lear denies it (ll. 264-8). The little that we see of the knights (ll. 51-75) shows them courteous, quiet and thoughtful. Much depends on the director of a production on this point.*
[243] disordered *disorderly*
     bold *insolent*
[245] Epicurism *extravagant indulgence (supposedly the mark of disciples of Epicurus)*
[247] graced *(by the presence of the king)*
[250] disquantity *reduce in quantity*
     train *followers*
[252] besort *be suitable for*

[259] Woe *woe to him (or her). But to whom is this applied? Superficially, it is addressed to Goneril. 'You had better repent of your conduct before it's too late'. Lear must, however, also be thinking of himself, determined to repent in time of his indulgence to Goneril, conscious that he repented too late of his harshness to Cordelia.*

Are lethargied— Ha! Waking? 'Tis not so!   230
  Who is it that can tell me who I am?
FOOL Lear's shadow.
LEAR I would learn that; for by the marks
  Of sovereignty, knowledge, and reason,
  I should be false persuaded I had daughters.
FOOL Which they will make an obedient father.
LEAR Your name, fair gentlewoman?
GONERIL This admiration, sir, is much o' th' savour
  Of other your new pranks. I do beseech you
  To understand my purposes aright.   240
  As you are old and reverend, should be wise.
  Here do you keep a hundred knights and squires –
  Men so disordered, so debauched and bold,
  That this our court, infected with their manners,
  Shows like a riotous inn. Epicurism and lust
  Makes it more like a tavern or a brothel
  Than a graced palace. The shame itself doth
    speak
  For instant remedy. Be then desired,
  By her that else will take the thing she begs,
  A little to disquantity your train;   250
  And the remainders, that shall still depend,
  To be such men as may besort your age,
  Which know themselves and you.
LEAR   Darkness and devils!
  Saddle my horses; call my train together!
  Degenerate bastard, I'll not trouble thee.
  Yet have I left a daughter.
GONERIL You strike my people, and your disordered
    rabble
  Make servants of their betters.

Enter ALBANY

LEAR Woe that too late repents! – O sir, are you
    come?

[263] the sea-monster *sea-monsters of legend*

[264] kite *bird of prey*

[267-8] in . . . name *with the most scrupulous attention live up to the honour of their reputation*

[268] most small fault *Cordelia's failure to respond was a small fault in comparison with Goneril's callous ingratitude; the fault is also small in comparison with its large effect in deranging Lear.*

[270-71] like . . . place *This painful image shows us Lear's consciousness of the deep unsettlement of his being. An 'engine' was any mechanical contrivance, but chiefly one used in sieges, or for torture. The rack is often thought of here. His 'frame of nature' is his natural disposition, with its capacity for true affection, seen as his own bodily structure being wrenched apart by a fiendish machine. Yet he realises that this painful derangement was caused by the ugly appearance of what he now sees in reality as a 'most small fault'.*

[273] this gate *his head*

[277] Nature . . . goddess *Nature here is not Edmund's deification of natural impulse, but 'great creating nature', the earth-mother*

[278] Suspend thy purpose *Lear's response to the lack of nature in Goneril is cruelly 'anti-nature' itself.*

[282] derogate *degraded*

[283] teem *become pregnant*

[284] spleen *malice*

[285] thwart disnatured *perverse, unnatural*

[287] cadent *falling*
fret *wear*

Is it your will? Speak, sir! – Prepare my horses.   260
Ingratitude, thou marble-hearted fiend,
More hideous when thou show'st thee in a child   *2nd reference*
Than the sea-monster!   *to animals*

ALBANY   Pray, sir, be patient.   *when insulting*

LEAR [*To* GONERIL] Detested kite, thou liest!   *animal daughters*
My train are men of choice and rarest parts,
That all particulars of duty know,
And in the most exact regard support
The worships of their name. O most small fault,
How ugly didst thou in Cordelia show,
Which, like an engine, wrenched my frame of   270
  nature
From the fixed place, drew from my heart all love,
And added to the gall. O Lear, Lear, Lear!
Beat at this gate that let thy folly in
                     [*Striking his head*
And thy dear judgement out! Go, go, my people.
                    [*Exeunt* KENT *and* KNIGHTS

ALBANY My lord, I am guiltless, as I am ignorant
Of what hath moved you.

LEAR   It may be so, my lord.
Hear, Nature; hear, dear goddess, hear!
Suspend thy purpose, if thou didst intend
To make this creature fruitful.
Into her womb convey sterility;   280
Dry up in her the organs of increase;
And from her derogate body never spring
A babe to honour her! If she must teem,
Create her child of spleen, that it may live
And be a thwart disnatured torment to her.
Let it stamp wrinkles in her brow of youth.
With cadent tears fret channels in her cheeks,
Turn all her mother's pains and benefits
To laughter and contempt, that she may feel
How sharper than a serpent's tooth it is   290
To have a thankless child! Away, away!   [*Exit*

[294-5] let . . . gives it *Goneril coolly treats Lear's outburst as a tantrum of old age, and tells Albany to let it have its course.*

[296] fifty . . . clap *This precise reduction is news to us.*

[300] perforce *unavoidably*

[301] make . . . them *give you the importance of being their ause*

[302] untented woundings *untreated wounds*

[304] Beweep this cause *if you weep for this matter*

[306] temper *prepare for use by softening*

[308] kind and comfortable *naturally affectionate and able to provide comfort*

[311-12] resume . . . cast off *'Shape' was regularly used for purely external appearance, such as is provided by clothes, theatrical costumes, or even disguise. Lear sees kingship as something you can take off and put on again.*

[313-4] partial . . . To *influenced in your favour by*

ALBANY Now, gods that we adore, whereof comes
    this?
GONERIL Never afflict yourself to know more of it,
    But let his disposition have that scope
    As dotage gives it.

Enter LEAR

LEAR What, fifty of my followers at a clap?
    Within a fortnight?
ALBANY   What's the matter, sir?
LEAR I'll tell thee. [*To* GONERIL] Life and death!
    I am ashamed
    That thou hast power to shake my manhood thus;
    That these hot tears, which break from me   300
      perforce,
    Should make thee worth them. Blasts and fogs
      upon thee!
    Th'untented woundings of a father's curse
    Pierce every sense about thee! Old fond eyes,
    Beweep this cause again, I'll pluck ye out,
    And cast you with the waters that you loose
    To temper clay. Yea, is't come to this?
    Ha! Let it be so. I have another daughter,
    Who I am sure is kind and comfortable.
    When she shall hear this of thee, with her nails
    She'll flay thy wolvish visage. Thou shalt find   310
    That I'll resume the shape which thou dost think
    I have cast off for ever.   [*Exit*
GONERIL   Do you mark that?
ALBANY I cannot be so partial, Goneril,
    To the great love I bear you –
GONERIL Pray you, content. What, Oswald, ho!
    [*To the* FOOL] You, sir, more knave than fool, after
      your master!
FOOL Nuncle Lear, nuncle Lear! Tarry, take the fool
    with thee.

[319–23] caught her . . . after   *All the endings would probably rhyme in Elizabethan pronunciation.*

---

[326] At point   *armed*

[327] buzz   *rumour*

[329] in mercy   *at his mercy*

[332] fear   . . taken   *be constantly afraid of being overtaken by harms*

[341] compact   *strengthen*

[345] attaxed   *to blame. This is an emendation: the Folio gives us 'at task', the Quarto has 'alapt' corrected to 'attaskt' (see p. 23).*

A fox, when one has caught her,
And such a daughter, 320
Should sure to the slaughter,
If my cap would buy a halter.
So the fool follows after. [*Exit*

GONERIL This man hath had good counsel! A
hundred knights?
'Tis politic and safe to let him keep
At point a hundred knights; yes, that on every
dream,
Each buzz, each fancy, each complaint, dislike,
He may enguard his dotage with their powers,
And hold our lives in mercy. Oswald, I say!

ALBANY Well, you may fear too far.

GONERIL   Safer than trust too far. 330
Let me still take away the harms I fear,
Not fear still to be taken. I know his heart.
What he hath uttered I have writ my sister.
If she sustain him and his hundred knights,
When I have showed th'unfitness –

Enter OSWALD

                    How now, Oswald?
What, have you writ that letter to my sister?

OSWALD Ay, madam.

GONERIL Take you some company and away to
horse.
Inform her full of my particular fear,
And thereto add such reasons of your own 340
As may compact it more. Get you gone,
And hasten your return. [*Exit* OSWALD
                    No, no, my lord,
This milky gentleness and course of yours
Though I condemn not, yet, under pardon,
You are much more attaxed for want of wisdom
Than praised for harmful mildness.

[Handwritten margin note: true reason for G wanting to get rid of high knights. Not because they are rowdy]

83

[350] th' event   *we'll wait and see how it turns out*

ACT ONE, scene 5

Lear, meditating on the wrong done to him by Goneril and regretting both the wrong he has done to Cordelia and also his division of the kingdom, begins to fear for his reason.

[1] Gloucester   *presumably the town. Some think Shakespeare meant 'Cornwall' (the duke). The geography of the play is very vague.*

[3] comes . . . demand   *may arise from any questions she has*

[9] kibes   *chilblains*

[11–12] thy . . . slip-shod   *you won't need slippers for your chilblains because you have no brains*

[15] kindly   (*1*) *with natural affection* (*2*) *in the way of her kind, cruelly*

      crab   *sour apple*

[18–19] She . . . crab   *Lear is only half-listening to the Fool, whose last remark needs no response. When Lear absently asks 'What canst tell?', the Fool impatiently explains the implication of what he has just said.*

[20] on's   *of his*

[22] side's   *side of his*

ALBANY How far your eyes may pierce I cannot tell:
　　Striving to better, oft we mar what's well.
GONERIL Nay, then –
ALBANY Well, well; th'event.　　　　　　　　[*Exeunt* 350

Scene 5. *Enter* LEAR, KENT *and* FOOL

LEAR Go you before to Gloucester with these letters.
　　Acquaint my daughter no further with anything you
　　know than comes from her demand out of the letter.
　　If your diligence be not speedy, I shall be there
　　afore you.
KENT I will not sleep, my lord, till I have delivered
　　your letter.　　　　　　　　　　　　　　　[*Exit*
FOOL If a man's brains were in's heels, were't not in
　　danger of kibes?
LEAR Ay, boy.　　　　　　　　　　　　　　　　10
FOOL Then I prithee be merry; thy wit shall not go
　　slip-shod.
LEAR Ha, ha, ha!
FOOL Shalt see thy other daughter will use thee
　　kindly; for, though she's as like this as a crab's like
　　an apple, yet I can tell what I can tell.
LEAR What canst tell, boy?
FOOL She will taste as like this as a crab does to a
　　crab. Thou canst tell why one's nose stands i'th'
　　middle on's face?　　　　　　　　　　　　　20
LEAR No.
FOOL Why, to keep one's eyes of either side's nose,
　　that what a man cannot smell out, he may spy
　　into.
LEAR I did her wrong.
FOOL Canst tell how an oyster makes his shell?
LEAR No.
FOOL Nor I neither; but I can tell why a snail has a
　　house.

[33] forget my nature   (*1*) *lose my paternal affection* (*2*) *lose my identity*

[36] seven stars   *in the constellation called the Pleiades*
     moe   *more*

[40] To . . . perforce   *to take the kingdom back again by force*

[47] in temper   *in my proper frame of mind*

LEAR Why? 30

FOOL Why, to put's head in; not to give it away to his daughters, and leave his horns without a case.

LEAR I will forget my nature. So kind a father! Be my horses ready?

FOOL Thy asses are gone about 'em. The reason why the seven stars are no moe than seven is a pretty reason.

LEAR Because they are not eight.

FOOL Yes, indeed; thou wouldst make a good fool.

LEAR To take't again perforce! Monster ingratitude! 40

FOOL If thou wert my fool, nuncle, I'd have thee beaten for being old before thy time.

LEAR How's that?

FOOL Thou shouldst not have been old till thou hadst been wise.

LEAR O, let me not be mad, not mad, sweet heaven! Keep me in temper; I would not be mad!

Fears his Jodgement is failing

Enter GENTLEMAN

How now! Are the horses ready?

GENTLEMAN Ready, my lord.

LEAR Come, boy. 50

FOOL She that's a maid now, and laughs at my departure,

Shall not be a maid long, unless things be cut shorter.

[*Exeunt*

ACT TWO, scene 1

A night-scene at Gloucester's castle. Edmund completes his scheme for discrediting and disinheriting Edgar. The main-plot and the sub-plot are linked, and the lines between the opposing parties in the play are drawn more clearly when Cornwall and Regan 'adopt' Edmund and identify Edgar as one of Lear's followers.

[1] Save   *God save*
[8] ear-bussing   *ear-kissing*

[10–11] wars . . . Albany   *These do not materialise though they are elsewhere in the play mentioned as being in the air. It was accepted in Elizabethan political thought that a division of rule such as Lear had made between Cornwall and Albany would inevitably lead to civil war.*

[15] The better   *so much the better*

[16] This . . . business   *their arrival means that they will inevitably become involved in his schemes*
[17] take   *take prisoner*
[18] queasy question   *ticklish nature*
[19] Briefness . . . work   *may speed and good fortune carry the day*

[21] watches   *is keeping awake, on the watch*
[22] Intelligence   *information*

[27] Upon his party   *on Cornwall's behalf. Edmund tries to give Edgar the impression that he has enemies everywhere.*
[28] Advise yourself   *consider*

ACT TWO

Scene 1. *Enter* EDMUND *and* CURAN, *from opposite sides*

EDMUND Save thee, Curan.

CURAN And you, sir. I have been with your father,
and given him notice that the Duke of Cornwall and
Regan his Duchess will be here with him this night.

EDMUND How comes that?

CURAN Nay, I know not. You have heard of the news
abroad, I mean the whispered ones, for they are yet
but ear-bussing arguments?

EDMUND Not I. Pray you, what are they?

CURAN Have you heard of no likely wars toward   10
'twixt the Dukes of Cornwall and Albany?

EDMUND Not a word.

CURAN You may do, then, in time. Fare you well,
sir.   [*Exit*

EDMUND The Duke be here tonight? The better! The
best!
This weaves itself perforce into my business.
My father hath set guard to take my brother,
And I have one thing, of a queasy question,
Which I must act. Briefness and fortune, work!
Brother, a word! Descend! Brother, I say!   20

Enter EDGAR

My father watches. O sir, fly this place!
Intelligence is given where you are hid.
You have now the good advantage of the night.
Have you not spoken 'gainst the Duke of Cornwall?
He's coming hither, now i'th' night, i'th' haste,
And Regan with him. Have you nothing said
Upon his party 'gainst the Duke of Albany?
Advise yourself.

[30] In cunning   *in pretence, as a plot*
[31] quit you well   *fight as well as you can*

[34–5] beget . . . endeavour   *make people think I fought more fiercely than I did*
[35–6] drunkards . . . sport   *An Elizabethan gallant might cut his arm and drink his blood as a toast to his mistress.*

[39] conjuring   *invoking by incantations*
[39–40] Mumbling . . . mistress   *character-blackening chosen to affect the superstitious Gloucester*

[42] Fled this way   *Edmund points in the wrong direction; he does not want Gloucester and Edgar to meet.*

[46] bend   *aim*

[48] in fine   *finally*
[49] how . . . stood   *with how much disgust I was opposed*

EDGAR   I am sure on't, not a word.
EDMUND I hear my father coming. Pardon me,
   In cunning I must draw my sword upon you.   30
   Draw, seem to defend yourself. Now quit you
      well –
   Yield! Come before my father. Light, ho! Here! –
   Fly, brother. – Torches, torches! – So; farewell.
                              [*Exit* EDGAR
   Some blood drawn on me would beget opinion
   Of my more fierce endeavour. I have seen
      drunkards
   Do more than this in sport.   [*Wounds his arm*
                              Father, father!
   Stop, stop! No help?

Enter GLOUCESTER, *and* SERVANTS *with torches*

GLOUCESTER   Now, Edmund, where's the villain?
EDMUND Here stood he in the dark, his sharp sword
      out,
   Mumbling of wicked charms, conjuring the moon
   To stand auspicious mistress.
GLOUCESTER   But where is he?   40
EDMUND Look, sir, I bleed.
GLOUCESTER   Where is the villain, Edmund?
EDMUND Fled this way, sir, when by no means he
      could –
GLOUCESTER Pursue him, ho! Go after. By no means
      what?
                              [*Exeunt some* SERVANTS
EDMUND Persuade me to the murder of your
      lordship.
   But that I told him the revenging gods
   'Gainst parricides did all the thunder bend,
   Spoke with how manifold and strong a bond
   The child was bound to th' father – sir, in fine,
   Seeing how loathly opposite I stood

[50] fell *deadly*

[52] unprovided *unprepared*
       latched *wounded*
[53] alarumed *aroused to battle*
[55] gasted *terrified*
[56–7] Let . . . uncaught *he will have to go into exile in another country to avoid capture*

[58] And . . . dispatch *and when he's found, kill him*

[59] arch *chief*

[62] to the stake *to be executed*
[63] death *will be put to death*

[65] pight *with fixed intent*
       curst speech *angry words*
[66] discover *reveal*
[67] unpossessing *unable to possess land by inheritance*
[68–70] would the reposal . . . faithed *that the placing of any trust (etc.) would make your words believed*

[72] character *handwriting (i.e. the letter)*
[73] suggestion *instigation*
       practice *evil scheming*
[74] make . . . world *turn everyone stupid*
[75] If . . . thought *if they don't think*
       profits . . . death *what you would gain by my death*
[76] pregnant . . . spurs *rich and powerful incitements*
[77] fastened *obdurate*
[78] got *begot*
       [Tucket within] *trumpet-call off-stage*

[80] ports *gates, ways out*

To his unnatural purpose, in fell motion   50
With his preparéd sword he charges home
My unprovided body, latched mine arm;
But when he saw my best alarumed spirits,
Bold in the quarrel's right, roused to th'encounter,
Or whether gasted by the noise I made,
Full suddenly he fled.
GLOUCESTER   Let him fly far,
Not in this land shall he remain uncaught;
And found – dispatch. The noble Duke my
     master,
My worthy arch and patron, comes tonight.
By his authority I will proclaim it,   60
That he which finds him shall deserve our thanks,
Bringing the murderous coward to the stake;
He that conceals him, death.
EDMUND When I dissuaded him from his intent,
And found him pight to do it, with curst speech
I threatened to discover him. He replied,
'Thou unpossessing bastard, dost thou think,
If I would stand against thee, would the reposal
Of any trust, virtue, or worth in thee
Make thy words faithed? No. What I should deny,   70
(As this I would – ay, though thou didst produce
My very character) I'd turn it all
To thy suggestion, plot, and damnéd practice;
And thou must make a dullard of the world,
If they not thought the profits of my death
Were very pregnant and potential spurs
To make thee seek it.'
GLOUCESTER   O strange and fastened villain!
Would he deny his letter, said he? I never got him.
                         [Tu et within
Hark, the Duke's trumpets! I know not why he
     comes.
All ports I'll bar, the villain shall not 'scape –   80
The Duke must grant me that. Besides, his picture

[84] natural boy *Gloucester seems to have swallowed some of Edmund's philosophy (see I. 2. 6–15). The natural child (illegitimate children were so called) being conceived by natural desire turns out to have more natural affection.*

[84–5] work . . . capable *organise the measures to enable you to inherit*

[91] my father's godson *Regan is quick to establish a relation between villainy and Lear*

[94] companion . . . knights *A further attempt to establish the case of the immorality of Lear's train; compare I. 4. 242–6.*

[97] consort *company*

[98] ill affected *evilly disposed*

[99] put him on *set him on to*

[100] expense and waste *squandering*

[106] childlike office *dutiful service proper for a son*

[107] bewray his practice *reveal his evil schemes*

I will send far and near, that all the kingdom
May have due note of him; and of my land,
Loyal and natural boy, I'll work the means
To make thee capable.

Enter CORNWALL, REGAN *and* ATTENDANTS

CORNWALL How now, my noble friend? Since I came
hither,
Which I can call but now, I have heard strange
news.
REGAN If it be true, all vengeance comes too short
Which can pursue th'offender. How dost, my lord?
GLOUCESTER O madam, my old heart is cracked, it's   90
cracked.
REGAN What, did my father's godson seek your life?
He whom my father named, your Edgar?
GLOUCESTER O lady, lady, shame would have it hid!
REGAN Was he not companion with the riotous
knights
That tended upon my father?
GLOUCESTER I know not, madam. 'Tis too bad, too bad!
EDMUND Yes, madam; he was of that consort.
REGAN No marvel, then, though he were ill affected.
'Tis they have put him on the old man's death,
To have th'expense and waste of his revenues.   100
I have this present evening from my sister
Been well informed of them, and with such
cautions
That, if they come to sojourn at my house,
I'll not be there.
CORNWALL   Nor I, assure thee, Regan.
Edmund, I hear that you have shown your father
A childlike office.
EDMUND   It was my duty, sir.
GLOUCESTER He did bewray his practice, and received
This hurt you see, striving to apprehend him.

[111] of doing harm *for the harm he might do*

[111-12] Make . . . please *carry out your own plans (for his capture) using my authority as you think fit*

[117] however else *however inadequate I may be in other respects*

[119] threading . . . night *threading our way through the darkness (as though it were the eye of a needle)*

[120] prize *importance*

[123] differences *disputes*

[124] answer . . . home *give my response away from home. Regan has been appealed to by both sides in the dispute. She has already made up her mind what her answer is, and she prefers to give it on neutral ground, where the claim on her hospitality is less.*

several messengers *messengers from each side*

[125] From . . . dispatch *are here waiting to be sent back*

[128] craves . . . use *demand immediate attention*

ACT TWO, scene 2

Follows directly the last scene; day dawns during the course of the scene. The two messengers we have just heard about meet, and Kent, still angry with Oswald for his contemptuous behaviour to the King, sets upon him. Cornwall stops the brawl and inflicts the humiliating punishment of the stocks on the King's messenger.

CORNWALL Is he pursued?

GLOUCESTER   Ay, my good lord.

CORNWALL If he be taken, he shall never more   110
  Be feared of doing harm. Make your own
      purpose,
  How in my strength you please. For you,
      Edmund,
  Whose virtue and obedience doth this instant
  So much commend itself, you shall be ours.
  Natures of such deep trust we shall much need;
  You we first seize on.

EDMUND   I shall serve you, sir,
  Truly, however else.

GLOUCESTER   For him I thank your Grace.

CORNWALL You know not why we came to visit you?

REGAN Thus out of season, threading dark-eyed
      night –
  Occasions, noble Gloucester, of some prize,   120
  Wherein we must have use of your advice.
  Our father he hath writ, so hath our sister,
  Of differences, which I best thought it fit
  To answer from our home. The several messengers
  From hence attend dispatch. Our good old friend,
  Lay comforts to your bosom, and bestow
  Your needful counsel to our businesses,
  Which craves the instant use.

GLOUCESTER   I serve you, madam.
  Your Graces are right welcome.

                              [*Flourish. Exeunt*

Scene 2. *Enter* KENT *and* OSWALD, *from opposite sides*

OSWALD Good dawning to thee, friend. Art of this
      house?

[2] Ay *Kent, who has recognised Oswald, has further cause for annoyance in the brisk condescension of the unobservant steward. He is willing to act the role Oswald suggests – of a lowly servant of Gloucester's.*

[4] mire *mud*

[8] Lipsbury pinfold *A pinfold is a pound for stray animals. There is no such place as Lipsbury; Kent makes it up, still pretending to be a humble and surly 'local'.*

[13] broken meats *leftovers*
[14] three-suited *with only three suits (possibly a sneer at these being the allowance for a servant)*
[15] hundred-pound *The valuation of his property is insufficient for him to rank as a gentleman, who lived off his land.*
     worsted-stocking *woollen, rather than the genteel silk*
[16] lily-livered *white-livered, hence, cowardly*
     action-taking *rushing to the shelter of the law*
     glass-gazing *always looking at himself in a mirror*
[17] super-serviceable *over-anxious to be 'at your service' (?)*
     finical *fussy*
[17–18] one-trunk-inheriting *heir to as much as will go in a trunk*
[18–19] be . . . service *act as a procurer if it were asked of you by your superior*
[23] thy addition *the titles I have given you*
[25] rail *pour abuse*

[31] sop o' th' moonshine *Although Kent is clearly indicating to Oswald that he's going to make mincemeat of him, the precise meaning of this phrase is not known.*
[32] cullionly *rascally*
     barber-monger *one who is always at the barber's*

[35] Vanity the puppet *Goneril is seen as the personification of wordly self-interest in a morality play performed as a puppet-show.*

KENT Ay.

OSWALD Where may we set out horses?

KENT I'th' mire.

OSWALD Prithee, if thou lov'st me, tell me.

KENT I love thee not.

OSWALD Why then, I care not for thee.

KENT If I had thee in Lipsbury pinfold, I would make
thee care for me.

OSWALD Why dost thou use me thus? I know thee   10
not.

KENT Fellow, I know thee.

OSWALD What dost thou know me for?

KENT A knave, a rascal, an eater of broken meats;
a base, proud, shallow, beggarly, three-suited,
hundred-pound, filthy worsted-stocking knave; a
lily-livered, action-taking, whoreson, glass-gazing,
super-serviceable, finical rogue; one-trunk-inheriting slave; one that wouldst be a bawd in way
of good service, and art nothing but the composition of a knave, beggar, coward, pandar, and   20
the son and heir of a mongrel bitch; one whom I
will beat into clamorous whining if thou deni'st
the least syllable of thy addition.

OSWALD Why, what a monstrous fellow art thou, thus
to rail on one that is neither known of thee nor
knows thee!

KENT What a brazen-faced varlet art thou, to deny
thou knowest me! Is it two days since I tripped up
thy heels and beat thee before the king? Draw, you
rogue; for, though it be night, yet the moon shines.   30
I'll make a sop o'th' moonshine of you, you
whoreson cullionly barber-monger. Draw!

> [*Drawing his sword*

OSWALD Away! I have nothing to do with thee.

KENT Draw, you rascal! You come with letters against
the king, and take Vanity the puppet's part against
the royalty of her father. Draw, you rogue, or I'll so

[37] carbonado your shanks *slash your legs (as though preparing meat for cooking)*

[37-8] Come your ways *come along with you*

[40] Strike ... Stand *Kent is trying to get Oswald to fight properly. First he won't draw his sword, then he won't strike. Finally, he won't stand, i.e. he tries to run away. Exasperated, Kent beats him.*

[41] neat *elegant*

[44] goodman boy *my fine young fellow*

[45] flesh ye *give you your first taste of fighting*

[50] difference *dispute*

[53] in thee *her part in making you*

[53-4] a tailor ... thee *he is nothing but what his clothes make him*

[59] two ... trade *To be still a beginner after two years in the trade indicates the length of apprenticeship in Elizabethan times and the high standards of craftsmanship.*

[62] at ... beard *in consideration of his age*

[63] zed ... letter *Unnecessary, because then little used in English, and not at all in Latin.*

[65] unbolted *unsifted (i.e. entire)*

[66] jakes *privy*

wagtail *(a bird) used abusively of a woman; here suggesting effeminacy*

carbonado your shanks! Draw, you rascal! Come
your ways!

OSWALD Help, ho! murder! help!

KENT Strike, you slave! Stand, rogue! Stand, you   40
neat slave! Strike!   [*Beating him*

OSWALD Help, ho! murder, murder!

Enter EDMUND, *with his rapier drawn*

EDMUND How now? What's the matter? Part!

KENT With you, goodman boy, if you please! Come,
I'll flesh ye; come on, young master!

Enter CORNWALL, REGAN, GLOUCESTER *and* SERVANTS

GLOUCESTER Weapons? Arms? What's the matter here?

CORNWALL Keep peace, upon your lives!
He dies that strikes again. What is the matter?

REGAN The messengers from our sister and the king!

CORNWALL What is your difference? Speak.   50

OSWALD I am scarce in breath, my lord.

KENT No marvel, you have so bestirred your valour.
You cowardly rascal, Nature disclaims in thee; a
tailor made thee.

CORNWALL Thou art a strange fellow; a tailor make
a man?

KENT A tailor, sir. A stone-cutter or a painter could
not have made him so ill, though they had been but
two years o'th'trade.

CORNWALL Speak yet, how grew your quarrel?   60

OSWALD This ancient ruffian, sir, whose life I have
spared
At suit of his grey beard –

KENT Thou whoreson zed, thou unnecessary letter!
My lord, if you will give me leave, I will tread this
unbolted villain into mortar and daub the wall of a
jakes with him. Spare my grey beard, you wagtail?

[71] **wear a sword** *The wearing of a sword in civil life was a social privilege: it is Kent's contention throughout that Oswald is a social pretender.*

[72–3] **smiling . . . atwain** *Shakespeare identifies the deepest evil with those who mask and hide their villainy beneath polished exteriors. Compare Hamlet's remark: 'One may smile, and smile, and be a villain'.*

[73] **holy cords** *those bonds between husband and wife, parent and child, king and subject, which were considered blessed by God*

　　atwain *in two*

[74] **intrince** *tightly knotted*

　　smooth *encourage by flattery*

[75] **rebel** *against proper self-control*

[77] **renege** *deny*

　　halcyon beaks *It was commonly believed that if you hung up a dead kingfisher, or halcyon, its beak would always point into the wind.*

[78] **gale and vary** *varying gale; i.e. every change of wind*

[80] **epileptic visage** *Oswald is smiling, and Kent implies that he looks as though he is having a fit.*

[81] **Smile you** *do you smile at*

[82–3] **Goose . . . Camelot** *Obscure: Sarum is Salisbury, and Camelot was the legendary capital of King Arthur.*

[88] **fault** *offence*

[89] **likes me not** *does not please me*

[90] **perchance** *perhaps*

[95] **affect** *assume out of vanity*

[96–7] **constrains . . . nature** *forces his mode of behaviour away from its natural path. Kent accuses Oswald of disguising his true nature under a cloak of obsequious gentility; Cornwall counters by claiming that it is Kent who is disguising his nature, under a cloak of bluntness and plainspeaking.*

[96] **garb** *mode of behaviour (not clothes)*

CORNWALL Peace, sirrah!
  You beastly knave, know you no reverence?
KENT Yes, sir; but anger hath a privilege.
CORNWALL Why art thou angry?   70
KENT That such a slave as this should wear a sword,
  Who wears no honesty. Such smiling rogues as
    these,
  Like rats, oft bite the holy cords atwain
  Which are too intrince t'unloose; smooth every
    passion
  That in the natures of their lords rebel,
  Bring oil to fire, snow to their colder moods;
  Renege, affirm, and turn their halcyon beaks
  With every gale and vary of their masters,
  Knowing nought (like dogs) but following.
  A plague upon your epileptic visage!   80
  Smile you my speeches, as I were a fool?
  Goose, if I had you upon Sarum Plain,
  I'd drive ye cackling home to Camelot.
CORNWALL What, art thou mad, old fellow?
GLOUCESTER How fell you out? Say that.
KENT No contraries hold more antipathy
  Than I and such a knave.
CORNWALL Why dost thou call him knave? What is
  his fault?
KENT His countenance likes me not.
CORNWALL No more perchance does mine, nor his,   90
  nor hers.
KENT Sir, 'tis my occupation to be plain.
  I have seen better faces in my time
  Than stands on any shoulder that I see
  Before me at this instant.
CORNWALL   This is some fellow,
  Who, having been praised for bluntness, doth
    affect
  A saucy roughness, and constrains the garb
  Quite from his nature. He cannot flatter, he!

[99] **An they . . . plain** *if they'll accept his statements, well and good; if not, he is not the one who is distorting things*

[102] **silly-ducking observants** *obsequious attendants foolishly bowing and scraping*

[103] **stretch . . . nicely** *A duty is an act of obeisance, so the image here is of fawning servants stretching themselves into ridiculous postures as they make their elaborate bows.*

[104] **verity** *truth*

[105] **Under th'allowance** *with the permission*

[107] **Phoebus** *the sun*

      front *forehead*

[108] **dialect** *manner of talking*

[111–12] **though . . . to't** *even though you hated me enough to beg me to become one (?)*

[116] **misconstruction** *misunderstanding*

[117] **compact** *in league with the king*

      flattering *encouraging by flattery*

[118] **being down, insulted** *when I was down he insulted me*

[119–20] **put . . . him** *claimed as much manhood as made a hero of him*

[121] **For . . . self-subdued** *for attacking a man who was not retaliating*

[122] **fleshment** *stimulation (as of a first taste of blood)*

[123–4] **None . . . fool** *all these rogues and cowards can fool Ajax (deceive him with their lies). Kent unwisely compares Cornwall with the Greek hero Ajax, whom Shakespeare thought of as a braggart, all brawn and no brain.*

[125] **reverend** *venerable (used here contemptuously)*

An honest mind and plain, he must speak truth!
An they will take it, so; if not, he's plain.
These kind of knaves I know which in this   100
  plainness
Harbour more craft and more corrupter ends
Than twenty silly-ducking observants
That stretch their duties nicely.
KENT Sir, in good faith, in sincere verity,
  Under th'allowance of your great aspect,
  Whose influence, like the wreath of radiant fire
  On flick'ring Phoebus' front –
CORNWALL   What mean'st by this?
KENT To go out of my dialect, which you dis-
  commend so much. I know, sir, I am no flatterer.
  He that beguiled you in a plain accent was a plain 110
  knave, which for my part I will not be, though I
  should win your displeasure to entreat me to 't.
CORNWALL What was th'offence you gave him?
OSWALD I never gave him any.
  It pleased the king his master very late
  To strike at me upon his misconstruction,
  When he, compact, and flattering his displeasure,
  Tripped me behind; being down, insulted, railed,
  And put upon him such a deal of man
  That worthied him, got praises of the king   120
  For him attempting who was self-subdued,
  And in the fleshment of this dread exploit
  Drew on me here again.
KENT   None of these rogues and cowards
  But Ajax is their fool.
CORNWALL   Fetch forth the stocks!
  You stubborn ancient knave, you reverend
    braggart,
  We'll teach you!
KENT   Sir, I am too old to learn.
  Call not your stocks for me; I serve the king,
  On whose employment I was sent to you.

[130] grace and person *the majesty of kingship and Lear as a man*

[136] colour *complexion*
[137] bring away *bring along*

[139] fault *offence*
[140] check *reprimand*

[141] contemnéd'st *most despicable*

[144] slightly valued *rated so cheaply*
[145] answer *be responsible for*

[148] following *attending to*

[152] rubbed *impeded*

You shall do small respect, show too bold malice
Against the grace and person of my master,   130
Stocking his messenger.
CORNWALL   Fetch forth the stocks!
As I have life and honour, there shall he sit till
noon.
REGAN Till noon? Till night, my lord, and all night
too.
KENT Why, madam, if I were your father's dog,
You should not use me so.
REGAN   Sir, being his knave, I will.
CORNWALL This is a fellow of the self-same colour
Our sister speaks of. Come, bring away the stocks.
                                   [*Stocks brought out*
GLOUCESTER Let me beseech your Grace not to do
so.
His fault is much, and the good king his master
Will check him for't. Your purposed low   140
correction
Is such as basest and contemnéd'st wretches
For pilferings and most common trespasses
Are punished with. The king must take it ill
That he, so slightly valued in his messenger,
Should have him thus restrained.
CORNWALL   I'll answer that.
REGAN My sister may receive it much more worse
To have her gentleman abused, assaulted,
For following her affairs. Put in his legs.

                    KENT *is put in the stocks*

[*To* CORNWALL] Come, my lord, away.
                    [*Exeunt all but* GLOUCESTER *and* KENT
GLOUCESTER I am sorry for thee, friend; 'tis the   150
duke's pleasure,
Whose disposition, all the world well knows,
Will not be rubbed nor stopped. I'll entreat for
thee.

                                                   107

[153] watched *been awake during the night*

[155] grow out at heels *suffer a decline (literally, get holes in his stockings)*

[156] Give *God give*

[158] approve *prove the truth of*
saw *saying*

[159-60] Thou . . . sun *Said of anyone going from somewhere protected to an insecure condition, from good to bad (the sun's heat being thought of as harsh).*

[161] Approach . . . globe *But Kent reflects that in spite of the proverb, you cannot do without the sun.*

[163-4] Nothing . . . misery *misery is almost the only thing to see miracles; i.e. it's only when one is wretched that one recognises the miraculous*

[166-7] find . . . state *The text seems corrupt here, and a line may have dropped out. The sense is that Cordelia will find time to rescue the kingdom from its abnormal situation ('enormous state').*

[168] o'er watched *tired through keeping awake*

[Sleeps] *Kent remains asleep in the stocks on stage during the forthcoming scene, though its location is elsewhere.*

ACT TWO, scene 3

A brief scene in which the fugitive Edgar plans to escape detection by disguising himself.

[1] proclaimed *publicly announced as a wanted man*

[2] happy . . . tree *good fortune of a hollow tree to hide in*

[3] port *gateway*

[5] attend my taking *keep watch to capture me*

[6] am bethought *I have it in mind*

[7-9] To take . . . beast *to adopt the vilest appearance, nearest to a beast, to which poverty, in its contempt for human dignity, ever reduced man*

KENT Pray do not, sir. I have watched, and travelled
    hard.
  Some time I shall sleep out, the rest I'll whistle.
  A good man's fortune may grow out at heels.
  Give you good morrow!
GLOUCESTER The duke's to blame in this; 'twill be
    ill taken.   [*Exit*
KENT Good king, that must approve the common
    saw,
  Thou out of heaven's benediction com'st
  To the warm sun!   160
  Approach, thou beacon to this under globe,
  That by thy comfortable beams I may
  Peruse this letter. Nothing almost sees miracles
  But misery. I know 'tis from Cordelia,
  Who hath most fortunately been informed
  Of my obscuréd course and shall find time
  From this enormous state, seeking to give
  Losses their remedies. All weary and o'erwatched,
  Take vantage, heavy eyes, not to behold
  This shameful lodging.   170
  Fortune, good night; smile once more; turn thy
    wheel.   [*Sleeps*

Scene 3. *Enter* EDGAR

EDGAR I heard myself proclaimed,
  And by the happy hollow of a tree
  Escaped the hunt. No port is free, no place
  That guard and most unusual vigilance
  Does not attend my taking. Whiles I may 'scape
  I will preserve myself; and am bethought
  To take the basest and most poorest shape
  That ever penury in contempt of man
  Brought near to beast. My face I'll grime with
    filth,

[10] elf *tangle (like a mischievous elf)*
[11] presented *exhibited*
    outface *defy*
[13] proof *example*
[14] Bedlam *see note to I. 2. 141*
[15] Strike *stick*
    mortified *dead to feeling*
[17] object *sight*
    low *humble*
[18] pelting *paltry*
[19] bans *curses*
[20] Turlygod *The meaning of this name is not known.*

[21] That's . . . am *there's a future in 'poor Tom'; I'm no
longer Edgar at all*

ACT TWO, scene 4

*Evening of the same day. Lear finds that Regan has no more
tenderness for him than Goneril had. The two sisters calmly
confront their king and father and try to reduce him to the
status of a meek dependant. Lear, driven about by the conflicting emotions of indignation, anger, self-pity, the desire for
affection, and the humiliating need of a home, becomes inarticu-
late with rage; with the crash of thunder overhead, his mind
gives way, and he rushes out into the storm. His daughters
coolly and self-righteously withdraw to shelter.*

[3–4] purpose . . . remove *intention to make this move*
[7] cruel *There is a pun on 'crewel', a coarse wool for stockings.*

[10] over-lusty at legs *given to running away*

[11] nether-stocks *stockings*

Blanket my loins, elf all my hairs in knots,   10
And with presented nakedness outface
The winds and persecutions of the sky.
The country gives me proof and precedent
Of Bedlam beggars who, with roaring voices,
Strike in their numbed and mortified bare arms
Pins, wooden pricks, nails, sprigs of rosemary;
And with this horrible object, from low farms,
Poor pelting villages, sheep-cotes, and mills,
Sometimes with lunatic bans, sometime with
    prayers,
Enforce their charity. 'Poor Turlygod, poor   20
    Tom!'
That's something yet! Edgar I nothing am.   [*Exit*

Scene 4. *Enter* LEAR, FOOL *and* GENTLEMAN

LEAR 'Tis strange that they should so depart from
    home,
And not send back my messenger.
GENTLEMAN   As I learned,
    The night before there was no purpose in them
    Of this remove.
KENT   Hail to thee, noble master!
LEAR Ha!
    Mak'st thou this shame thy pastime?
KENT   No, my lord.
FOOL Ha, ha! He wears cruel garters. Horses are
    tied by the heads, dogs and bears by th' neck, mon-
    keys by th' loins, and men by th' legs. When a
    man's over-lusty at legs, then he wears wooden   10
    nether-stocks.
LEAR What's he that hath so much thy place mistook
    To set thee here?
KENT   It is both he and she,
    Your son and daughter.

[24] upon respect   *deliberately (with second meaning of 'against the respect due to a king')*

[25] Resolve me   *make clear to me*

with . . . haste   *as fast as you can without unseemliness*

[27] coming from us   *considering that you were the king's messenger*

[29–30] that . . . kneeling   *where I showed my respect by kneeling*

[30] reeking   *steaming with heat*

[31] stewed   *soaked with sweat*

[33] spite of intermission   *even though he was interrupting me*

[34] presently   *immediately*

[35] meiny   *retinue*

[41] Displayed so saucily   *showed himself off so insolently*

[42] Having . . . me   *acting more as a man of honour than one of good sense*

[44] worth   *deserving of*

[46] Winter's . . . way   *the worst is still to come (wild geese fly south at the start of the winter)*

LEAR No.

KENT Yes.

LEAR No, I say.

KENT I say yea.

LEAR No, no, they would not.

KENT Yes, they have. 20

LEAR By Jupiter, I swear no!

KENT By Juno, I swear ay!

LEAR   They durst not do't,
  They could not, would not do't; 'tis worse than
    murder
  To do upon respect such violent outrage.
  Resolve me with all modest haste which way
  Thou mightst deserve or they impose this usage,
  Coming from us.

KENT   My lord, when at their home
  I did commend your highness' letters to them,
  Ere I was risen from the place that showed
  My duty kneeling, came there a reeking post, 30
  Stewed in his haste, half breathless, panting forth
  From Goneril his mistress salutations;
  Delivered letters, spite of intermission,
  Which presently they read; on whose contents
  They summoned up their meiny, straight took
    horse,
  Commanded me to follow and attend
  The leisure of their answer, gave me cold looks;
  And meeting here the other messenger,
  Whose welcome I perceived had poisoned mine –
  Being the very fellow which of late 40
  Displayed so saucily against your Highness –
  Having more man than wit about me, drew.
  He raised the house with loud and coward cries.
  Your son and daughter found this trespass worth
  The shame which here it suffers.

FOOL Winter's not gone yet if the wild geese fly that
  way.

113

[47-54] Fathers . . . year *Penniless fathers have uncaring ('blind') children. Rich fathers have affectionate children. Fortune like a whore opens her door only when there's money around – but you will have plenty of dollars – that is, 'dolours' (griefs).*

[55-6] mother . . . Hysterica passio *Two names for the same complaint, a feeling of suffocation or choking, thought to rise from the belly*

[57] Thy element *the element you belong to (earth, air, fire or water)*

[64] An *if*

[67-8] We'll . . .winter *In the fable, the ant (unlike the grasshopper) prudently laid up stocks in the summer because it is impossible to collect food in the winter. The Fool means Kent should learn how to look after himself, and not toil where there's nothing to be got.*

[68-71] All . . . stinking *i.e. even if you are so blind that you can't see what is happening, your other senses ought to tell you*

[77] sir *man*

[81] But . . . tarry *The Fool doesn't really believe in his own worldly wisdom. He may be a fool but he's not a knave.*

> Fathers that wear rags
> > Do make their children blind,
> But fathers that bear bags
> > Shall see their children kind.   50
> Fortune, that arrant whore,
> > Ne'er turns the key to th' poor.

But for all this thou shalt have as many dolours for thy daughters as thou canst tell in a year.

LEAR O, how this mother swells up toward my heart! Hysterica passio! Down, thou climbing sorrow, Thy element's below. Where is this daughter?

KENT With the earl, sir, here within.

LEAR Follow me not; stay here.   [*Exit*

GENTLEMAN Made you no more offence but what you   60 speak of?

KENT None.
How chance the king comes with so small a number?

FOOL An thou hadst been set i'th' stocks for that question, thou'dst well deserved it.

KENT Why, fool?

FOOL We'll set thee to school to an ant, to teach thee there's no labouring i'th' winter. All that follow their noses are led by their eyes but blind men, and there's not a nose among twenty but can smell him that's   70 stinking. Let go thy hold when a great wheel runs down a hill, lest it break thy neck with following; but the great one that goes upward, let him draw thee after. When a wise man gives thee better counsel, give me mine again. I would have none but knaves use it, since a fool gives it.

> That sir which serves and seeks for gain
> > And follows but for form,
> Will pack when it begins to rain
> > And leave thee in the storm.   80
> But I will tarry, the fool will stay
> > And let the wise man fly.

Fool-comedy may, help to lift poem from despair

[87] Deny   *refuse*

[88] fetches   *tricks*

[89] images   *signs*
      flying off   *desertion*

[91] quality   *temperament*

[93] confusion!   *destruction! (the strongest in Lear's crescendo
of curses, consigning the objects of his wrath to perdition)*

[100] commands her service   *Here the Folio reads 'commands,
tends, service'.*

[104–5] Infirmity . . . bound   *when we are ill, we always neglect
those duties which we have to attend to when we are in good health*

The knave turns fool that runs away;
  The fool no knave, perdy.
KENT Where learned you this, fool?
FOOL Not i'th'stocks, fool!

Enter LEAR, *with* GLOUCESTER

LEAR Deny to speak with me? They are sick, they
  are weary,
  They have travelled all the night? Mere fetches.
    Ay,
  The images of revolt and flying off.
  Fetch me a better answer.
GLOUCESTER   My dear lord,   90
  You know the fiery quality of the duke,
  How unremovable and fixed he is
  In his own course.
LEAR   Vengeance! plague! death! confusion!
  Fiery? What quality? Why, Gloucester,
    Gloucester,
  I'ld speak with the Duke of Cornwall and his wife.
GLOUCESTER Well, my good lord, I have informed
  them so.
LEAR Informed them? Dost thou understand me,
  man?
GLOUCESTER Ay, my good lord.
LEAR The king would speak with Cornwall; the
  dear father
  Would with his daughter speak, commands her   100
    service.
  Are they informed of this? My breath and blood!
  Fiery? the fiery duke? Tell the hot duke that –
  No, but not yet. May be he is not well:
  Infirmity doth still neglect all office
  Whereto our health is bound. We are not ourselves
  When nature, being oppressed, commands the
    mind

(margin, handwritten) Fool functions as chorus

[108] my . . . will   *my hastier impulse*

[110] Death . . . state!   *death to my royalty! (an odd curse in the circumstances)*

[112] remotion   *keeping out of the way*
[113] practice   *scheming*
          forth   *(from the stocks)*
[115] presently   *immediately*

[117] cry . . . death   *screams sleep into extinction (?)*

[120] cockney   *silly woman*
[121] put . . . alive   *She is making an eel-pie, and she hasn't realised that the eels should be killed first. 'Paste' is dough or pastry.*
          knapped   *rapped*
[122] coxcombs   *heads*
[123] wantons   *'you naughty things'*
[124] buttered his hay   *Dishonest stable-men used to grease a horse's teeth so that he wouldn't eat the hay provided. The brother's mistaken act of kindness would have the same effect. The purpose of both these ridiculous anecdotes is the same: Lear complains of his condition but it's his own fault for being stupid enough to think his deed a kindness.*

[129–30] divorce . . . adultress   *consider myself divorced from your dead mother, and let her body lie solitary in the royal sepulchre as an adultress (since Regan's unkindness would prove that he was not her father)*

[132] naught   *wicked*
[133] like a vulture   *Prometheus was tortured by a vulture gnawing at his liver.*

To suffer with the body. I'll forbear,
And am fallen out with my more headier will
To take the indisposed and sickly fit
For the sound man. [*Looking on* KENT] Death on   110
  my state! Wherefore
Should he sit here? This act persuades me
That this remotion of the duke and her
Is practice only. Give me my servant forth.
Go tell the duke and 's wife I'd speak with them
Now, presently. Bid them come forth and hear me,
Or at their chamber door I'll beat the drum
Till it cry sleep to death.
GLOUCESTER I would have all well betwixt you. [*Exit*
LEAR O me, my heart! My rising heart! But down!
FOOL Cry to it, nuncle, as the cockney did to the eels 120
when she put 'em i' th' paste alive. She knapped
'em o' th' coxcombs with a stick and cried 'Down,
wantons, down!' 'Twas her brother that in pure
kindness to his horse buttered his hay.

      Enter GLOUCESTER, *with* CORNWALL, REGAN
             and SERVANTS

LEAR Good morrow to you both.
CORNWALL   Hail to your Grace!

        KENT *here set at liberty*

REGAN I am glad to see your highness.
LEAR Regan, I think you are. I know what reason
  I have to think so; if thou shouldst not be glad,
  I would divorce me from thy mother's tomb,
  Sepulchring an adultress. [*To* KENT] O, are you   130
  free?
  Some other time for that. – Beloved Regan,
  Thy sister's naught. O Regan, she hath tied
  Sharp-toothed unkindness, like a vulture, here.
                [*Points to his heart*

[135] quality   *nature*

[136–8] I have . . . duty   *I hope you are more ignorant of her worth than she is of her duty. Shakespeare has in fact said the opposite of what he intended, by using 'scant' (come short in).*

[145–6] Nature . . . confine   *i.e. you are at the absolute limit of your natural life*

[146] confine   *limited area*

[147] discretion . . . state   *understanding person who knows your condition*

[151] becomes the house   *is fitting for the head of the royal house*

[152–4] Dear . . . food   *For a second time (compare I. 4. 227–31), Lear acts a little playlet which unwittingly displays his real situation.*

[153] Age is unnecessary   *old people are not needed*

[154] vouchsafe   *kindly grant*

[157] abate   *deprived*

[161] top   *head*

young bones   *The phrase could refer to an unborn child, but in the context Lear is clearly concerned with Goneril herself, his child*

[162] taking airs   *pestilential vapours*

[163] nimble   *swift*

I can scarce speak to thee – thou'lt not believe
With how depraved a quality – O Regan!
REGAN I pray you, sir, take patience. I have hope
  You less know how to value her desert
  Than she to scant her duty.
LEAR   Say? How is that?
REGAN I cannot think my sister in the least
  Would fail her obligation. If, sir, perchance   140
  She have restrained the riots of your followers,
  'Tis on such ground and to such wholesome end
  As clears her from all blame.
LEAR My curses on her!
REGAN   O sir, you are old.
  Nature in you stands on the very verge
  Of his confine. You should be ruled and led
  By some discretion that discerns your state
  Better than you yourself. Therefore I pray you
  That to our sister you do make return.
  Say you have wronged her.
LEAR   Ask her forgiveness?   150
  Do you but mark how this becomes the house!
  'Dear daughter, I confess that I am old; [*Kneeling*
  Age is unnecessary; on my knees I beg
  That you'll vouchsafe me raiment, bed, and food!'
REGAN Good sir, no more. These are unsightly tricks.
  Return you to my sister.
LEAR [*Rising*]   Never, Regan!
  She hath abated me of half my train,
  Looked black upon me, struck me with her
    tongue
  Most serpent-like upon the very heart.
  All the stored vengeances of heaven fall   160
  On her ingrateful top. Strike her young bones,
  You taking airs, with lameness!
CORNWALL   Fie, sir, fie!
LEAR You nimble lightnings, dart your blinding
  flames

[165] fen-sucked *sucked from the fens*
[166] To fall and blister her *to fall on her and cover her with blisters. (The text is uncertain at this point.)*

[169] tender-hefted *gently-framed*

[173] scant my sizes *reduce my allowances*
[174] oppose the bolt *bolt the door*

[176] offices *duties*
[177] Effects *manifestations*

[181] approves *confirms*

[183] easy-borrowed *not his own, but on loan from Goneril*

ACT TWO, SCENE FOUR

Into her scornful eyes! Infect her beauty,
You fen-sucked fogs, drawn by the powerful sun
To fall and blister her!

REGAN   O the blest gods!
So will you wish on me when the rash mood is
   on.

LEAR No, Regan, thou shalt never have my curse.
Thy tender-hefted nature shall not give
Thee o'er to harshness. Her eyes are fierce; but   170
   thine
Do comfort and not burn. 'Tis not in thee
To grudge my pleasures, to cut off my train,
To bandy hasty words, to scant my sizes,
And in conclusion to oppose the bolt
Against my coming in. Thou better know'st
The offices of nature, bond of childhood,
Effects of courtesy, dues of gratitude.
Thy half o' th' kingdom hast thou not forgot,
Wherein I thee endowed.

REGAN   Good sir, to th' purpose.

LEAR Who put my man i' th' stocks?

                           [*Tucket within*

CORNWALL   What trumpet's that? 180

REGAN I know't – my sister's. This approves her
   letter,
That she would soon be here.

Enter OSWALD

                   Is your lady come?

LEAR This is a slave whose easy-borrowed pride
Dwells in the sickly grace of her he follows.
Out, varlet, from my sight!

CORNWALL   What means your Grace?

LEAR Who stocked my servant? Regan, I have good
   hope
Thou didst not know on't.

[187–90] O heavens . . . part *What is the force of the repeated 'if'? Does Lear begin to doubt whether his gods support the traditional social hierarchy, or is he using rhetorical language to stress his confidence that the gods are indeed on his side? Whatever our answer, we may think that there is a tendency here (which the cynical Edmund called 'the policy and reverence of age' I. 2. 47) to imagine a divine order which is comforting to authority.*

[189] Allow *approve of*

[194] that . . . finds *that a person lacking judgement considers to be so*

[195] sides *the frame of the body*

[196] Will . . . hold? *i.e. how is it that with the burning volcano inside him, his physical frame still holds together?*

[198] much less advancement *i.e. a worse punishment*

[204] entertainment *reception*

[207] wage *contend*

[209] Necessity's . . . pinch *This also is what he chooses.*

[210] hot-blooded *amorous*

[212] knee · *kneel before*

squire-like . . . beg *as though I were a servant, beg him to support me*

[214] sumpter *beast of burden*

Enter GONERIL

     Who comes here? O heavens,
If you do love old men, if your sweet sway
Allow obedience, if you yourselves are old,
Make it your cause. Send down and take my part! 190
[*To* GONERIL] Art not ashamed to look upon this
 beard?
O Regan! will you take her by the hand?
GONERIL Why not by th' hand, sir? How have I
 offended?
All's not offence that indiscretion finds
And dotage terms so.
LEAR   O sides, you are too tough!
Will you yet hold? How came my man i'th' stocks?
CORNWALL I set him there, sir; but his own
 disorders
Deserved much less advancement.
LEAR   You? Did you?
REGAN I pray you, father, being weak, seem so.
If, till the expiration of your month,   200
You will return and sojourn with my sister,
Dismissing half your train, come then to me.
I am now from home, and out of that provision
Which shall be needful for your entertainment.
LEAR Return to her? and fifty men dismissed?
No, rather I abjure all roofs, and choose
To wage against the enmity o' th' air,
To be a comrade with the wolf and owl –
Necessity's sharp pinch! Return with her?
Why, the hot-blooded France, that dowerless took 210
Our youngest born, I could as well be brought
To knee his throne and, squire-like, pension beg
To keep base life afoot. Return with her?
Persuade me rather to be slave and sumpter
To this detested groom. [*Pointing at* OSWALD

[216–23] *The rapid succession of moods in Lear is noticeable here. In the first line, his fear of the volcano within him is evident. In the second and third lines, he for a moment masters his rising anger, and achieves a rather stagey loftiness. This is succeeded by the self-pitying 'But yet thou art my flesh', at which the bottled-up fury can no longer be restrained, until he pulls himself up again with the tone of injured forgiveness of 'But I'll not chide thee'.*

[222] embossed carbunéle *inflamed tumour (like a boil)*

[225] thunder-bearer *Jupiter*

[232] mingle . . . passion *intersperse cool reason among your passionate outcries*

[235] avouch *affirm*

[237] sith that *since*
     charge *expense*

[240] amity *friendship*

[243] slack *neglect*

[244] control *rebuke*

GONERIL   At your choice, sir.

LEAR I prithee, daughter, do not make me mad.
  I will not trouble thee, my child; farewell.
  We'll no more meet, no more see one another.
  But yet thou art my flesh, my blood, my
    daughter –
  Or rather a disease that's in my flesh,   220
  Which I must needs call mine. Thou art a boil,
  A plague-sore, or embosséd carbuncle
  In my corrupted blood. But I'll not chide thee;
  Let shame come when it will, I do not call it.
  I do not bid the thunder-bearer shoot,
  Nor tell tales of thee to high-judging Jove.
  Mend when thou canst; be better at thy leisure.
  I can be patient; I can stay with Regan,
  I and my hundred knights.

REGAN   Not altogether so.
  I looked not for you yet, nor am provided   230
  For your fit welcome. Give ear, sir, to my sister;
  For those that mingle reason with your passion
  Must be content to think you old, and so –
  But she knows what she does.

LEAR   Is this well spoken?

REGAN I dare avouch it, sir. What! fifty followers?
  Is it not well? What should you need of more?
  Yea, or so many, sith that both charge and
    danger
  Speak 'gainst so great a number? How in one
    house
  Should many people, under two commands,
  Hold amity? 'Tis hard, almost impossible.   240

GONERIL Why might not you, my lord, receive
    attendance
  From those that she calls servants, or from mine?

REGAN Why not, my lord? If then they chanced to
    slack ye,
  We could control them. If you will come to me

[247] notice *recognition*

[249] Made . . . depositaries *entrusted my estate to you to watch over*

[250] kept a reservation *made a condition*

[254] well-favoured *good-looking*

[258] twice her love *A telling illustration of how Lear still judges affection, as he does personal status, by a standard of material quantity.*

[262] reason . . . need *don't try to make exact calculations of need*

[262–3] Our . . . superfluous *the meanest possessions of the destitute are superfluous to their real needs*

[264–5] Allow . . . beast's *if you are going to argue on the basis simply of what natural man needs, you are putting man's life on the level of the beasts*

[266–8] If only . . . warm *if your only requirement in dressing yourselves was warmth, you wouldn't need the gorgeous clothes you are wearing – which don't keep you warm anyway. Lear implies that his daughters recognise a need (in wearing fine clothes) which has nothing to do with the reasoned need they are trying to impose on him.*

[268] But . . . need *Lear breaks off because he does not know – yet – what true need is. His idea of need is exactly the same as that which he sarcastically attributes to his daughters in their love of gorgeous clothes. He believes that a man is different from the beasts because he has non-natural needs: possessions, followers, titles, respect, which establish one's dignity and being. He suddenly becomes aware of the falsity of his position.*

(For now I spy a danger), I entreat you
To bring but five and twenty; to no more
Will I give place or notice.

LEAR I gave you all –

REGAN   And in good time you gave it.

LEAR Made you my guardians, my depositaries,
But kept a reservation to be followed   250
With such a number. What! must I come to you
With five and twenty? Regan, said you so?

REGAN And speak 't again, my lord; no more with
    me.

LEAR Those wicked creatures yet do look well-
favoured
When others are more wicked; not being the worst
Stands in some rank of praise. [*To* GONERIL] I'll
    go with thee.
Thy fifty yet doth double five and twenty,
And thou art twice her love.

GONERIL   Hear me, my lord.
What need you five and twenty, ten, or five,
To follow in a house where twice so many   260
Have a command to tend you?

REGAN   What need one?

LEAR O reason not the need! Our basest beggars
Are in the poorest things superfluous.
Allow not nature more than nature needs,
Man's life is cheap as beast's. Thou art a lady;
If only to go warm were gorgeous,
Why, nature needs not what thou gorgeous
    wear'st,
Which scarcely keeps thee warm. But for true
    need –
You heavens, give me that patience, patience I
    need!
You see me here, you gods, a poor old man,   270
As full of grief as age, wretched in both.
If it be you that stirs these daughters' hearts

129

[273] fool . . . much *don't make me such a fool*

[283] flaws *fragments*
[284] Or ere *before*

[287] bestowed *accommodated*
[288] from rest *i.e. into discomfort*

[289] taste *experience (the result of)*
[290] For . . . particular *as regards himself*

[291] purposed *determined*

[295] calls to horse *gives orders for his horses. Shakespeare seems to forget the horses.*

[296] he . . . himself *he makes his own decisions*

Against their father, fool me not so much
To bear it tamely; touch me with noble anger,
And let not women's weapons, water drops,
Stain my man's cheeks. No, you <u>unnatural</u> hags,
I will have such revenges on you both
That all the world shall – I will do such things –
What they are yet I know not, but they shall be
The terrors of the earth! You think I'll weep;   280
No, I'll not weep.
I have full cause of weeping,   *[Storm and tempest*
                              but this heart
Shall break into a hundred thousand flaws
Or ere I'll weep. O Fool, I shall go mad!
                    [Exeunt LEAR, GLOUCESTER, KENT *and* FOOL
CORNWALL Let us withdraw; 'twill be a storm.
REGAN This house is little; the old man and's people
  Cannot be well bestowed.
GONERIL 'Tis his own blame; hath put himself from
  rest,
  And must needs taste his folly.
REGAN For his particular, I'll receive him gladly,   290
  But not one follower.
GONERIL   So am I purposed.
  Where is my lord of Gloucester?
CORNWALL Followed the old man forth. He is
  returned.

Enter GLOUCESTER

GLOUCESTER The king is in high rage.
CORNWALL   Whither is he going?
GLOUCESTER He calls to horse, but will I know not
  whither.
CORNWALL 'Tis best to give him way; he leads
  himself.
GONERIL My lord, entreat him by no means to stay.

[299] ruffle *bluster*

[304] incense *provoke*
[305] have . . . abused *listen to bad advice*

GLOUCESTER Alack, the night comes on, and the
   bleak winds
  Do sorely ruffle. For many miles about
  There's scarce a bush.

REGAN   O sir, to wilful men   300
  The injuries that they themselves procure
  Must be their schoolmasters. Shut up your doors.
  He is attended with a desperate train,
  And what they may incense him to, being apt
  To have his ear abused, wisdom bids fear.

CORNWALL Shut up your doors, my lord; 'tis a wild
   night.
  My Regan counsels well. Come out o' th' storm.
                         [Exeunt

ACT THREE, scene 1

In the storm and darkness, one of Lear's attendants meets Kent and tells him about the King. Kent gives him the news that a French army has landed, and sends his companion to Dover to greet Cordelia and tell her what has happened. This is an awkward scene; it exists in very different versions in the Quarto and Folio, and the text given here is a patchwork of the two.

[2] minded   *with a mind*

[4] Contending with   *competing with (rather than 'struggling against')*

[6] main   *land*

[7] things . . . cease   *the universal order of things might be transformed or else come to an end*

[8] eyeless   *blind*

[9] make . . . of   *treat as worthless*

[10] little . . . man   *This is the common idea of man as a microcosm, or little world, that copies the structure of the great universe.*

[12] cub-drawn   *sucked dry by her cubs*
       couch   *remain in its lair (in preference to hunting for food)*

[14] unbonneted   *hatless*

[15] bids . . . all   *tells whoever has a mind to, to appropriate everything. He who has been so concerned about apportioning out his kingdom is now totally indifferent to who owns what.*

[16] outjest   *conquer by jesting*

[17] heart-struck   *i.e. which have smitten his heart*

[18] warrant . . . note   *assurance of my knowledge of you*

[19] Commend   *entrust*
       dear   *important*

[22] great stars   *important destiny*

[23] seem no less   *seem no other than the servants they pretend to be*

[24] speculations   *'eyes'*

ACT THREE

Scene I. *The storm continues. Enter* KENT *and a*
GENTLEMAN, *from opposite sides*

KENT Who's there besides foul weather?
GENTLEMAN One minded like the weather, most
    unquietly.
KENT I know you. Where's the King?
GENTLEMAN Contending with the fretful elements;
    Bids the wind blow the earth into the sea,
    Or swell the curlèd waters 'bove the main,
    That things might change or cease; tears his white
      hair,
    Which the impetuous blasts with eyeless rage
    Catch in their fury and make nothing of;
    Strives in his little world of man to out-storm   10
    The to-and-fro-conflicting wind and rain.
    This night, wherein the cub-drawn bear would
      couch,
    The lion and the belly-pinchèd wolf
    Keep their fur dry, unbonneted he runs,
    And bids what will take all.
KENT   But who is with him?
GENTLEMAN None but the Fool, who labours to
    outjest
    His heart-struck injuries.
KENT   Sir, I do know you,
    And dare upon the warrant of my note
    Commend a dear thing to you. There is division,
    Although as yet the face of it is covered   20
    With mutual cunning, 'twixt Albany and Cornwall,
    Who have – as who have not, that their great stars
    Throned and set high? – servants, who seem no
      less,
    Which are to France the spies and speculations

[25] Intelligent *having knowledge*

[26] snuffs *resentments*
packings *plots*

[27] hard . . . borne *stern control which they have exercised*

[29] furnishings *the external appearances. There is a bad join in the text here between a passage given only in the Folio, and another given only in the Quarto.*

[30] power *army*

[31] scattered *divided*

[32] feet *footing*

[33–4] at point . . . banner *about to show their banner openly, i.e. declare themselves*

[35] on . . . far *you dare trust my credibility to such an extent*

[37] making . . . report *for giving a correct report*

[38] bemadding *maddening*

[39] plain *complain*

[40] of blood and breeding *nobly born and nurtured*

[41] assurance *certainty*

[42] office *duty*

[45] out-wall *exterior (he is still disguised)*

[48] fellow *companion*

[52] to effect *in importance*

[53–4] your pain . . . way *your kind labour should be in that direction. One of several things which are not clear in this scene is why the Gentleman, who gives no reason why he has left the King, should now be sent to search for him, as well as being sent off to Dover.*

Intelligent of our state. What hath been seen,
Either in snuffs and packings of the Dukes,
Or the hard rein which both of them hath borne
Against the old kind King: or something deeper
Whereof perchance these are but furnishings –
But true it is from France there comes a power   30
Into this scattered kingdom, who already,
Wise in our negligence, have secret feet
In some of our best ports and are at point
To show their open banner. Now to you:
If on my credit you dare build so far
To make your speed to Dover, you shall find
Some that will thank you, making just report
Of how unnatural and bemadding sorrow
The King hath cause to plain.
I am a gentleman of blood and breeding,   40
And from some knowledge and assurance offer
This office to you.
GENTLEMAN I will talk further with you.
KENT   No, do not.
  For confirmation that I am much more
  Than my out-wall, open this purse and take
  What it contains. If you shall see Cordelia
  (As fear not but you shall), show her this ring,
  And she will tell you who your fellow is
  That yet you do not know. Fie on this storm!
  I will go seek the King.   50
GENTLEMAN Give me your hand. Have you no more
    to say?
KENT Few words, but, to effect, more than all yet –
  That when we have found the King (in which
    your pain
  That way, I'll this) he that first lights on him
  Holla the other.   [*Exeunt on opposite sides*

proper order has been broken

137

ACT THREE, scene 2

Lear, bare-headed and drenched, cries out to the gale to obliterate a world which is unjust because it opposes him. Then, in a moment of insight, he hears in the wind, rain, and thunder an apocalyptic voice challenging the values of the world he has known, unmasking the secret sinners in their secure places.

[2] cataracts *deluge of water from the sky*

    hurricanoes *Shakespeare seems to have thought of hurricanes as waterspouts.*

[3] cocks *weathercocks on top of the steeples*

[4] sulphurous *Sulphur, or brimstone, was popularly associated with thunder and lightning.*

    thought-executing *May mean either 'carrying out Jove's thoughts', or 'acting as swift as thought'.*

[5] Vaunt-couriers *heralds*

[7] Strike . . . world *flatten the round world; 'thick rotundity' also suggests pregnancy*

[8] moulds *(by which all creatures are given shape)*

    germens *seeds*

[10] court . . . water *A derisive term for flattery.*

[14] Rumble thy bellyful *Lear ignores the Fool, and goes on addressing the storm. 'Rumble' could be applied equally to distant thunder or wind in the bowels.*

[16] tax *charge*

[18] subscription *allegiance*

[21] servile ministers *Lear thinks of himself as slave to the storm, but then calls the storm a slave to his daughters.*

[23] high-engendered battles *armies formed in the skies*

[25–6] good head-piece *(1) protection for his head (2) wisdom ('a good head on his shoulders')*

[27–30] *He who is keener on fornication than on getting a house for himself will end up as a lousy beggar; marriage for beggars is casual sex-relations rather than building up a home.*

[27] codpiece *the flap covering the crotch in male garments, but here meaning the sexual organ*

Scene 2. *The storm continues. Enter* LEAR *and* FOOL

LEAR Blow, winds, and crack your cheeks! rage!
    blow!
  You cataracts and hurricanoes, spout
  Till you havè drenched our steeples, drowned the
    cocks!
  You sulphurous and thought-executing fires,
  Vaunt-couriers of oak-cleaving thunderbolts,
  Singe my white head! And thou, all-shaking
    thunder,
  Strike flat the thick rotundity o'th' world,
  Crack Nature's moulds, all germens spill at once
  That makes ingrateful man!
FOOL O nuncle, court holy water in a dry house is   10
  better than this rain-water out o' door. Good
  nuncle, in; ask thy daughters blessing! Here's a
  night pities neither wise men nor fools.
LEAR Rumble thy bellyful! Spit, fire! spout, rain!
  <u>Nor rain, wind, thunder, fire are my daughters</u>.
  <u>I tax not you, you elements, with unkindness</u>;
  <u>I never gave you kingdom, called you children</u>;
  <u>You owe me no subscription</u>. Then let fall
  Your horrible pleasure. <u>Here I stand your slave</u>,
  <u>A poor, infirm, weak, and despised old man</u>.   20
  <u>But yet I call you servile ministers</u>,
  <u>That will with two pernicious daughters join</u>
  <u>Your high-engendered battles 'gainst a head</u>
  <u>So old and white as this. O, ho! 'tis foul</u>!
FOOL He that has a house to put's head in has a good
  head-piece.
        The codpiece that will house
        Before the head has any,
        The head and he shall louse:
        So beggars marry many.   30

[31–4] The man ... wake *He who prefers things of small worth shall suffer from those unworthy things in the end.*

[35–6] For ... glass *This is not related to what the Fool has been saying. Perhaps, finding himself growing sententious, he clowns this solemn saying with a wink at the women in the audience.*
        made ... glass *practised poses before a mirror*

[40–41] here's ... fool *but which is which, he leaves others to decide*

[44] Gallow *terrify*

[45] keep *remain inside*

[48] carry *endure*

[49–51] Let ... now *Lear has previously personified the storm itself; now he sees it as the instrument of the gods to terrify and expose the real sinners.*

[50] pudder *hubbub*

[53] Unwhipped of *unpunished by*

[53–5] Hide ... incestuous *The murderer, the perjurer, and the man who has committed incest, revealed in the lightning, are told they had better hide.*

[54] simular of virtue *pretender to chastity*

[55] Caitiff *wretch*

[56] covert ... seeming *the disguise of decent appearances (literally, hidden and decent false-appearance)*

[57] practised on *schemed against*
        Close *secret*

[58] Rive *split open*
        continents *containers*

[58–9] cry ... grace *beg mercy of these terrifying accusers ('summoners' brought offenders to ecclesiastical courts)*

[59–60] I am ... sinning *One of the pinnacles of Lear's vision; the outward show of personal niceness and social acceptability now seems to him to fester with hidden sin. But he asks himself where in this new valuation he himself stands. He recognises his guilt, that he is a sinner; but he recognises also that he is not one of those criminals he has just talked of – in fact he is one of their targets. A sinner, yes, but 'more sinned against than sinning'. He neither excuses nor pities himself.*

The man that makes his toe
    What he his heart should make
Shall of a corn cry woe,
    And turn his sleep to wake.
For there was never yet fair woman but she made
mouths in a glass.

Enter KENT

LEAR No, I will be the pattern of all patience;
  I will say nothing.

KENT Who's there?

FOOL Marry, here's grace and a codpiece; that's a wise 40
man and a fool.

KENT Alas, sir, are you here? <u>Things that love night</u>
<u>Love not such nights as these.</u> The wrathful skies
Gallow the very wanderers of the dark
And make them keep their caves. Since I was man,
Such sheets of fire, such bursts of horrid thunder,
Such groans of roaring wind and rain, I never
Remember to have heard. Man's nature cannot
  carry
Th'affliction, nor the fear.

LEAR   Let the great gods,
That keep this dreadful pudder o'er our heads, 50
Find out their enemies now. Tremble, thou
  wretch
That hast within thee undivulgéd crimes
Unwhipped of justice. Hide thee, thou bloody
  hand,
Thou perjured, and thou simular of virtue
That art incestuous. Caitiff, to pieces shake,
That under covert and convenient seeming
Has practised on man's life. Close pent-up guilts,
Rive your concealing continents, and cry
These dreadful summoners grace. <u>I am a man</u>
<u>More sinned against than sinning.</u>

He doesn't deserve so
much punishment. He has
sinned against natural
order

[67] scanted *insufficient*

My wits . . . turn *After his great appeal to the gods, Lear seems exhausted and bewildered. For the first time in this scene, he notices the Fool.*

[70–71] The art . . . precious *He begins to learn about true need (compare II. 4. 262–68). He had formerly said, in his ignorance, that beggars didn't need even their poorest possessions. Destitution teaches him what is really precious.*

[74–7] *The Fool sings another piece of the sad and cryptic ballad which Feste sang at the end of* Twelfth Night; *the burden of both Fools is the need to put up with a world that is against you all the time.*

[79] a brave . . . courtesan *a fine old night for streetwalkers. The Fool now plays to the audience; he adopts a heavy role as archaic prophet. It is a particularly clever prophecy, he claims at the end (ll. 95–6), because it is not going to be pronounced until the time of Merlin (who in the legendary chronology came after the days of Lear). The prophecy is a cunning mixture of things that were actually happening in Elizabethan times or could never happen. It is based upon some rhymes which Elizabethans thought were by Chaucer.*

[81] more . . . matter *have a lot to say but few valuable ideas*

[83] nobles . . . tutors *when proud aristocrats are reduced to taking employment as tutors in the families of the working-men whom they now exploit*

[84] No . . . suitors *when the only heretics to be burned are wenches' suitors – because they are faithless; but the jest is that the suitors may be 'burned' in a different sense of the word, i.e. infected with venereal disease*

[88] to throngs *among crowds*

[89] tell . . . field *count their money in public*

[90] bawds . . . build *It was a common libel that women made fortunes out of vice, then turned pious and used the money for charitable ends.*

[91–2] Then shall . . . confusion *In so far as the 'prophecies' are happening now, England ('the realm of Albion') is already in confusion; in so far as they are unrealisable ideals, there would certainly be confusion of the present state if they were to come about.*

142

KENT   Alack, bare-headed? 60
   Gracious my lord, hard by here is a hovel;
   Some friendship will it lend you 'gainst the
      tempest.
   Repose you there, while I to this hard house
   (More harder than the stones whereof 'tis raised,
   Which even but now, demanding after you,
   Denied me to come in) return, and force
   Their scanted courtesy.

LEAR   My wits begin to turn.
   Come on, my boy. How dost, my boy? Art cold?
   I am cold myself. Where is this straw, my fellow?
   <u>The art of our necessities is strange,</u>   70
   <u>And can make vile things precious.</u> Come, your
      hovel.
   Poor fool and knave. I have one part in my heart
   That's sorry yet for thee.

FOOL [*Sings*]
      He that has and a little tiny wit –
         With heigh-ho, the wind and the rain –
      Must make content with his fortunes fit,
         Though the rain it raineth every day.

LEAR True, boy. Come, bring us to this hovel.
                           [*Exeunt* LEAR *and* KENT

FOOL This is a brave night to cool a courtesan! I'll
   speak a prophecy ere I go: 80
     When priests are more in word than matter,
     When brewers mar their malt with water,
     When nobles are their tailors' tutors,
     No heretics burned, but wenches' suitors,
     When every case in law is right,
     No squire in debt nor no poor knight,
     When slanders do not live in tongues,
     Nor cutpurses come not to throngs,
     When usurers tell their gold i'th' field,
     And bawds and whores do churches build   90
     Then shall the realm of Albion

the confusion is present [handwritten marginal note]

143

[93–4] Then . . . feet *These things are happening now – the bad things; when the good things happen, we shall actually be behaving in the proper manner.*

ACT THREE, scene 3

Gloucester, realising the extent of the attack on Lear, and receiving news which indicates that the issue is likely to come to the conflict of arms, sees where his loyalty lies, but makes the fatal mistake of confiding in Edmund.

[3] pity *show pity to (in deeds)*

[8] Go to *that's enough*
[9] worse *more serious (referring to the invasion)*

[11] closet *private chest*

[13] home *thoroughly*
    part . . . footed *the first contingent of an army has already established a foothold*
[14] incline to *lend our support to*
    look *seek*
    privily *secretly*

[20] toward *impending*
[21] forbid thee *which you were forbidden to show (to Lear)*

[23] deserving *action deserving a reward*

Come to great confusion;
Then comes the time, who lives to see 't,
That going shall be used with feet.
This prophecy Merlin shall make, for I live before
his time.   [*Exit*

Scene 3. *Enter* GLOUCESTER *and* EDMUND

GLOUCESTER Alack, alack, Edmund, I like not this unnatural dealing. When I desired their leave that I
might pity him, they took from me the use of mine
own house, charged me on pain of perpetual displeasure neither to speak of him, entreat for him, or
any way sustain him.

EDMUND Most savage and unnatural!

GLOUCESTER Go to; say you nothing. There is division
between the Dukes, and a worse matter than that.
I have received a letter this night – 'tis dangerous to   10
be spoken – I have locked the letter in my closet.
These injuries the King now bears will be revenged
home. There is part of a power already footed. We
must incline to the King. I will look him and privily
relieve him. Go you and maintain talk with the
Duke, that my charity be not of him perceived; if he
ask for me, I am ill and gone to bed. If I die for it
(as no less is threatened me), the King, my old
master, must be relieved. There is strange things
toward, Edmund; pray you be careful.   [*Exit* 20

EDMUND This courtesy, forbid thee, shall the Duke
Instantly know, and of that letter too.
This seems a fair deserving, and must draw me
That which my father loses – no less than all.
The younger rises when the old doth fall.   [*Exit*

When Lear gives up throne, gives up position as father

145

ACT THREE, scene 4

Lear's further glimpses of a re-valued world emerge strangely mixed up with bursts of self-pity and signs of increasing madness. The brilliant acting of Edgar as a naked and mad beggar gives the king a new vision of basic humanity.

[3] nature *human nature*

[Storm still] *This direction is from the Folio, and indicates that the sound effects for the storm continue (intermittently) throughout the scene.*

[4] Wilt . . . heart *It is Kent's courtesy and concern for his comfort that Lear fears will make him break down. He has scores to settle in the storm – whatever they may be. He needs rest, but to relax from his scarcely-defined purpose is to admit defeat. The longed-for kindness would, he feels, be fatal now.*

[8] fixed *firmly placed (in his mind)*

[11–12] When . . . delicate *if the mind is not occupied with anxieties, the body has time to be sensitive*

[14] filial *belonging to a daughter or son*

[15–16] Is it . . . to't *This violent image of self-laceration shows how strong the bond of the family is in Lear's mind. But in these few lines it is the old Lear who speaks, conscious mainly of the obligations of others to himself.*

[16] home *to the fullest extent*

[18] shut me out *Self-pity blurs the truth that he left of his own free will.*

[20] frank *generous*

[24–5] This . . . more *Lear has just said that he doesn't notice the storm because of the distress in his mind; now he says exactly the opposite.*

Scene 4. *Enter* LEAR, KENT *and* FOOL

KENT Here is the place, my lord; good my lord,
   enter:
   The tyranny of the open night's too rough
   For nature to endure.
                              [*Storm still*
LEAR   Let me alone.
KENT Good my lord, enter here.
LEAR   Wilt break my heart?
KENT I had rather break mine own. Good my lord,
   enter.
LEAR Thou think'st 'tis much that this contentious
   storm
   Invades us to the skin. So 'tis to thee;
   But where the greater malady is fixed,
   The lesser is scarce felt. Thou'dst shun a bear;
   But if thy flight lay toward the roaring sea,   10
   Thou'dst meet the bear i'th' mouth. When the
   mind's free,
   The body's delicate; this tempest in my mind
   Doth from my senses take all feeling else
   Save what beats there – filial ingratitude!
   Is it not as this mouth should tear this hand
   For lifting food to 't? But I will punish home!
   No, I will weep no more. In such a night
   To shut me out? Pour on; I will endure.
   In such a night as this? O Regan, Goneril!
   Your old kind father whose frank heart gave all!   20
   O, that way madness lies; let me shun that!
   No more of that.
KENT   Good my lord, enter here.
LEAR Prithee go in thyself, seek thine own ease.
   This tempest will not give me leave to ponder
   On things would hurt me more. But I'll go in.

[27] I'll pray   *His sudden vision of 'houseless poverty' turns his thoughts outwards from self to others, and from outcry to prayer.*

[29] bide   *endure*

[31] looped . . . raggedness   *i.e. their clothes have loop-holes and window-holes in them*

[33] Take . . . pomp   *let those in authority take a medicine to purge themselves of their pride*

[35] shake the superflux   *distribute excess possessions*

[37] Fathom and half   *He's a sailor taking soundings.*

[43] grumble   *mutter*

[45] Away   *keep clear*
        foul fiend   *the devil*
[46] Through . . . winds   *presumably a line from an old song*
[48] Didst . . . daughters   *All wretchedness is now attributed to filial ingratitude.*

[*To the* FOOL] In boy, go first. You houseless
  poverty—
Nay, get thee in; I'll pray, and then I'll sleep—
                        [*Exit* FOOL
Poor naked wretches, whereso'er you are,
That bide the pelting of this pitiless storm,
How shall your houseless heads and unfed sides,   30
Your looped and windowed raggedness, defend
  you
From seasons such as these? O, I have ta'en
Too little care of this! Take physic, pomp;
Expose thyself to feel what wretches feel,
That thou mayst shake the superflux to them
And show the heavens more just.
EDGAR [*Within*] Fathom and half, fathom and half!
  Poor Tom!

Enter FOOL

FOOL Come not in here, nuncle, here's a spirit.
  Help me, help me!   40
KENT Give me thy hand. Who's there?
FOOL A spirit, a spirit! He says his name's poor Tom.
KENT What art thou that dost grumble there
  i'th' straw?
  Come forth!

Enter EDGAR, *disguised as a madman*

EDGAR Away! The foul fiend follows me!
  Through the sharp hawthorn blow the winds.
  Humh! Go to thy bed and warm thee.
LEAR Didst thou give all to thy daughters? And art
  thou come to this? Pathetic, seeing only betrayal of daughters
EDGAR Who gives anything to poor Tom? whom the   50 as bringing
  foul fiend hath led through fire and through flame, man to
  through ford and whirlpool, o'er bog and quagmire; this.

[53–4] *The devil has tried to tempt him to the great sin of suicide by setting the instruments near him: knives, a noose, poison.*

[54] pew   *chair*

  ratsbane   *rat poison*

[55–6] ride . . . bridges   *He has been tempted to risk his life by riding a high-stepping horse over the narrowest bridge.*

[56] course   *hunt*

[57] five wits   *understanding, imagination, perception, judgement, memory*

[58] Bless thee from   *God preserve thee from*

[58–9] star-blasting   *being under the malign influence of a star*

[59] taking   *infection*

[64] reserved   *kept back*

[66] pendulous   *hanging over us*

[67] fated   *directed by destiny*

  light   *alight*

[69] subdued nature   *reduced his being*

[72] have . . . flesh   *'have' must mean 'receive', since Lear's remark concerns rejected fathers being made to suffer physically.*

[73] Judicious   *appropriate*

[73–4] 'Twas . . . daughters   *The idea that sexual desire is sinful, and that we therefore deserve any suffering our children bring us, occurs elsewhere in the play, most notably in V. 3. 171–2. See Introduction, pages 21–22.*

[74] pelican   *The young pelicans were supposed to attack the parents.*

[75] Pillicock   *Lear's talk of begetting, and the sound of the word 'pelican', make Edgar bring out this childish name for the penis.*

[77–8] This . . . madmen   *It is rare to get a 'straight' remark from the Fool. He is perhaps taken aback by the last sally of Edgar's, which is so exactly his own brand of fooling. Does he recognise that Edgar is an artist, rather than what he pretends to be? At any rate, he feels the air too full of non-reason to add his own quota, and during the rest of the scene he speaks only once.*

[80] commit not   *do not commit adultery*

[82] proud array   *fine clothes*

[85] gloves   *the favours of his women-friends*

that hath laid knives under his pillow, and halters
in his pew; set ratsbane by his porridge; made him
proud of heart, to ride on a bay trotting horse over
four-inched bridges, to course his own shadow for a
traitor. Bless thy five wits! Tom's a-cold. O, do de,
do de, do de. Bless thee from whirlwinds, star-
blasting, and taking! Do poor Tom some charity,
whom the foul fiend vexes. There could I have him   60
now – and there – and there again – and there!

[*Storm still*

LEAR What, has his daughters brought him to this
pass?
Couldst thou save nothing? Wouldst thou give 'em
all?

FOOL Nay, he reserved a blanket; else we had been all
shamed.

LEAR Now all the plagues that in the pendulous air
Hang fated o'er men's faults light on thy daughters!

KENT He hath no daughters, sir.

LEAR Death, traitor! Nothing could have subdued
nature
To such a lowness but his unkind daughters.   70
Is it the fashion that discarded fathers
Should have thus little mercy on their flesh?
Judicious punishment! 'Twas this flesh begot
Those pelican daughters.

EDGAR Pillicock sat on Pillicock Hill.
Alow! alow, loo, loo!

FOOL This cold night will turn us all to fools and
madmen.

EDGAR Take heed o'th' foul fiend. Obey thy parents,
keep thy word justly, swear not, commit not with   80
man's sworn spouse, set not thy sweet heart on
proud array. Tom's a-cold.

LEAR What hast thou been?

EDGAR A servingman! proud in heart and mind;
that curled my hair, wore gloves in my cap, served

[91] out-paramoured the Turk *had more women than the Sultan of Turkey has in his harem*

[92] light of ear *immoral in what he would listen to*

[94] prey *marauding; seeking prey*

[94–5] Let not . . . woman *do not allow a midnight visitation from a woman to make you surrender your heart to her*

[96] plackets *slits in petticoats*

[99–100] Says . . . trot by *These are fragments thrown together in a lunatic way; what they are fragments of is uncertain.*

[101] answer *confront*

[102] extremity *extreme severity*

[102–3] Is man no more than this? *See Introduction, page 11.*

[103–4] Thou owest . . . *He has borrowed nothing from the animals.*

[105] cat *civet cat*

[106] sophisticated *adulterated (by the addition of what they have borrowed from the animals)*

[106–7] Unaccommodated man *man who is not fitted out for a non-natural existence*

[108] forked *two-legged*
        lendings *clothes (lent him by the animals)*

[110] naughty *wicked*

[112] wild *uncultivated, hence barren*

[115] Flibbertigibbet *the name of a demon which Shakespeare found in Samuel Harsnett's book,* Declaration of Egregious Popish Impostures

[116] curfew . . . first cock *dusk . . . dawn*

[116–17] web and the pin *cataract*

[117] squinies *causes to squint*

the lust of my mistress' heart, and did the act of
darkness with her; swore as many oaths as I spake
words, and broke them in the sweet face of heaven;
one that slept in the contriving of lust, and waked to
do it. Wine loved I deeply, dice dearly, and in   90
woman out-paramoured the Turk. False of heart,
light of ear, bloody of hand; hog in sloth, fox in
stealth, wolf in greediness, dog in madness, lion in
prey. Let not the creaking of shoes nor the rustling
of silks betray thy poor heart to woman. Keep thy
foot out of brothels, thy hand out of plackets, thy pen
from lenders' books, and defy the foul fiend.
Still through the hawthorn blows the cold wind,
Says suum, mun, nonny.
Dolphin my boy, boy! – sessa! let him trot by.   100

[Storm still

LEAR Thou wert better in a grave than to answer with
thy uncovered body this extremity of the skies. Is
man no more than this? Consider him well. Thou
owest the worm no silk, the beast no hide, the sheep
no wool, the cat no perfume. Ha! Here's three on's
are sophisticated: thou art the thing itself. Unaccommodated man is no more but such a poor, bare,
forked animal as thou art. Off, off, you lendings!
Come, unbutton here!

[Starts to tear off his clothes

FOOL Prithee, nuncle, be contented; 'tis a naughty   110
night to swim in!

Enter GLOUCESTER *with a torch*

Now a little fire in a wild field were like an old
lecher's heart – a small spark, all the rest on's body
cold. Look, here comes a walking fire.
EDGAR This is the foul Flibbertigibbet. He begins at
curfew, and walks till first cock. He gives the web
and the pin, squinies the eye, and makes the harelip;

[120] S'Withold   *St Withold, an old English saint and protector against demons*

        footed   *marched across*

        'old   *wold, open country*

[121] Nightmare   *demon who causes nightmares*

        fold   *offspring (?)*

[122] alight   *come down (?)*

[123] her troth plight   *pledge her word*

[124] aroint thee   *get thee gone*

[130] wall-newt . . . water   *the lizard and the newt*

[132] sallets   *salads*

[133] ditch-dog   *dog dead in a ditch*

        mantle   *slimy covering*

[134] standing   *stagnant*

[134] tithing   *parish. Vagabonds found begging were liable to be whipped and sent to their own parish or last residence.*

[136] who hath had   *i.e. in better times*

[139–40] But mice . . . year   *(adapted from a popular medieval romance)*

[141] Smulkin   *another name for a demon taken from Harsnett's book*

[144] Prince of Darkness   *the devil*

[144–5] Modo . . . Mahu   *more names from Harsnett*

[146] flesh and blood   *children*

[147] gets   *begets*

[149] suffer   *allow me*

mildews the white wheat, and hurts the poor
creature of earth.

    S'Withold footed thrice the 'old: 120
    He met the Nightmare and her nine fold;
      Bid her alight
      And her troth plight –
    And aroint thee, witch, aroint thee!

KENT How fares your grace?

LEAR What's he?

KENT Who's there? What is't you seek?

GLOUCESTER What are you there? Your names?

EDGAR Poor Tom, that eats the swimming frog, the
toad, the tadpole, the wall-newt and the water; that 130
in the fury of his heart, when the foul fiend rages,
eats cow-dung for sallets, swallows the old rat and
the ditch-dog, drinks the green mantle of the
standing pool; who is whipped from tithing to
tithing, and stocked, punished, and imprisoned;
who hath had three suits to his back, six shirts to
his body,
    Horse to ride, and weapon to wear;
    But mice and rats and such small deer
    Have been Tom's food for seven long year.   140
Beware my follower. Peace, Smulkin; peace, thou
fiend!

GLOUCESTER What, hath your Grace no better
    company?

EDGAR The Prince of Darkness is a gentleman! Modo
he's called, and Mahu.

GLOUCESTER Our flesh and blood, my lord, is grown
    so vile,
That it doth hate what gets it.

EDGAR Poor Tom's a-cold.

GLOUCESTER Go in with me. My duty cannot suffer
  T'obey in all your daughters' hard commands.   150
  Though their injunction be to bar my doors
  And let this tyrannous night take hold upon you,

[155] philosopher   *one who knows the secrets of nature*

[156] What . . . thunder   *In III. 2 Lear interpreted the thunder in a number of ways, seeing it partly as an expression of divine anger, and as an accompaniment of the disturbance in his own world. He wants someone to tell him authoritatively what, if anything, the gods have to do with the turmoil he observes and suffers.*

[158] learned Theban   *philosopher of Thebes (the allusion is unclear)*

[159] What . . . study?   *what is it that you study?*

[160] prevent   *forestall*

[168] outlawed . . . blood   *disinherited*

[169] late   *recently*

[172] cry you mercy   *please excuse me*

[179] soothe   *humour*

Yet have I ventured to come seek you out
And bring you where both fire and food is ready.

LEAR First let me talk with this philosopher.
What is the cause of thunder?

KENT Good my lord, take his offer; go into th' house.

LEAR I'll talk a word with this same learned Theban.
What is your study?

EDGAR How to prevent the fiend, and to kill vermin. 160

LEAR Let me ask you one word in private.

KENT Importune him once more to go, my lord.
His wits begin t' unsettle.

GLOUCESTER   Canst thou blame him?

[Storm still

His daughters seek his death. Ah, that good Kent!
He said it would be thus, poor banished man!
Thou sayest the King grows mad; I'll tell thee,
  friend,
I am almost mad myself. I had a son,
Now outlawed from my blood; he sought my life
But lately, very late. I loved him, friend,
No father his son dearer. True to tell thee,   170
The grief hath crazed my wits. What a night's
  this!
I do beseech your Grace –

LEAR   O, cry you mercy, sir.
Noble philosopher, your company.

EDGAR Tom's a-cold.

GLOUCESTER In, fellow, there, into th' hovel; keep
  thee warm.

LEAR Come, let's in all.

KENT   This way, my lord.

LEAR   With him!
I will keep still with my philosopher.

KENT Good my lord, soothe him; let him take the
  fellow.

GLOUCESTER Take him you on.

KENT Sirrah, come on; go along with us.   180

157

[182] Athenian   *no longer Theban, but still Greek*

[184] Child . . . came   *This magical line may be a fragment, but the work it comes from is not known. 'Child' is a young nobleman not yet knighted; Roland was companion to Charlemagne.*

[185] His word was still   *his motto was always*

[185-6] Fie . . . man   *Edgar switches to the story of Jack the Giant-Killer.*

ACT THREE, scene 5

Edmund betrays his father, with consummate smugness.

[3] censured   *judged*

[3-4] nature . . . loyalty   *affection for his father . . . loyalty to the state*

[4] something . . me   *rather worries me*

[8-9] provoking . . . himself   *i.e. Gloucester's qualities deserve punishment and may have provoked Edgar, though Edgar must be bad to entertain thoughts of murder.*

[11] repent . . . just   *regret acting justly*

[12] approves   *proves*
    intelligent party to   *informed supporter of*

[13] advantages   *underhand gaining of superior positions*

[18-19] True . . . Gloucester   *Even if the information of the French invasion is false, Gloucester is guilty of intriguing with a foreign power, and on his death as a traitor, the title will come to Edmund.*

[21] comforting   *lending assistance to*

[23] persever   *(accent on second syllable) persevere*

LEAR Come, good Athenian.
GLOUCESTER No words, no words; hush!
EDGAR Child Roland to the dark tower came.
His word was still 'Fie, foh, and fum.
I smell the blood of a British man.'

[*Exeunt*

Scene 5. *Enter* CORNWALL *and* EDMUND

CORNWALL I will have my revenge ere I depart his house.
EDMUND How, my lord, I may be censured, that nature thus gives way to loyalty, something fears me to think of.
CORNWALL I now perceive it was not altogether your brother's evil disposition made him seek his death; but a provoking merit, set awork by a reproveable badness in himself.
EDMUND How malicious is my fortune, that I must 10 repent to be just! This is the letter he spoke of, which approves him an intelligent party to the advantages of France. O heavens! that this treason were not, or not I the detector!
CORNWALL Go with me to the Duchess.
EDMUND If the matter of this paper be certain, you have mighty business in hand.
CORNWALL True or false, it hath made thee Earl of Gloucester. Seek out where thy father is, that he may be ready for our apprehension. 20
EDMUND [*Aside*] If I find him comforting the King, it will stuff his suspicion more fully. [*To* CORNWALL] I will persever in my course of loyalty, though the conflict be sore between that and my blood.
CORNWALL I will lay trust upon thee; and thou shalt find a dearer father in my love.

[*Exeunt*

ACT THREE, scene 6

This scene takes place in a roughly furnished room in some out-building on Gloucester's estate. With the help of the Fool and the disguised Edgar, Lear stages a trial of his daughters. This 'arraignment' is a subtle three-part motet of mad voices, eerie, and very moving.

[2] piece out   *add something to*

[5] impatience   *The word is used in a strict sense, inability to endure annoyance or injury. Were Lear able to tolerate his daughters' behaviour, he would not be mad.*

[6] Frateretto   *another demon taken from Harsnett's book*

[6–7] Nero . . . darkness   *Nero is taken as the extreme example of those who commit crimes against their own family, for he murdered his mother. Such sinners will spend eternity in hell.*

[10] gentleman or a yeoman   *A gentleman had enough land to live off the income; a yeoman owned land but had to work for his living.*

[15] thousand   *(devils?)*

[16] hizzing   *hissing*

[20] arraign them   *bring them to trial*
     straight   *immediately*

[22] sapient   *wise*

[23] he   *the devil*

[24–5] Want'st . . . madam   *meaning uncertain; the text may be at fault here; we have only the Quarto to rely on for this passage*

[26] Come . . . me   *a line from a song; 'burn' means brook.*

[26–8] Her boat . . . thee   *The Fool improvises the next three lines of the song; the indecent undermeaning of the leaky boat is that Bessy is diseased.*

[31] nightingale   *Poor Tom's view of Edgar's singing voice.*
     Hoppedance   *another devil from Harsnett*

Scene 6. *Enter* KENT *and* GLOUCESTER

GLOUCESTER Here is better than the open air; take it
thankfully. I will piece out the comfort with what
addition I can. I will not be long from you.
KENT All the power of his wits have given way to his
impatience. The gods reward your kindness!

[*Exit* GLOUCESTER

ability to take pressures and sorrows

Enter LEAR, EDGAR *and* FOOL

EDGAR Frateretto calls me, and tells me Nero is an
angler in the lake of darkness. Pray, innocent, and
beware the foul fiend.
FOOL Prithee, nuncle, tell me whether a madman be
a gentleman or a yeoman.   10
LEAR A king, a king!
FOOL No, he's a yeoman that has a gentleman to his
son; for he's a mad yeoman that sees his son a gentle-
man before him.
LEAR To have a thousand with red burning spits
Come hizzing in upon 'em!
EDGAR The foul fiend bites my back.
FOOL He's mad that trusts in the tameness of a wolf,
a horse's health, a boy's love, or a whore's oath.
LEAR It shall be done; I will arraign them straight.   20
[*To* EDGAR] Come sit thou here, most learnèd justice.
[*To the* FOOL] Thou sapient sir, sit here. Now, you
she-foxes!
EDGAR Look where he stands and glares! Want'st
thou eyes at trial, madam? [*Sings*]
        Come o'er the burn, Bessy, to me.
FOOL [*Sings*]   Her boat hath a leak,
                And she must not speak
        Why she dares not come over to thee.
EDGAR The foul fiend haunts poor Tom in the voice   30
of a nightingale. Hoppedance cries in Tom's belly

[32] Croak not   *Poor Tom's stomach is rumbling.*

[34] amazed   *not so much 'surprised' as 'in a state of bewilder-ment'. In this scene, as in many of the previous scenes, Lear will often be seen to stand as though in a daze, oblivious of what others are say-ing, occupied with his own intolerable thoughts.*

[37] robéd   *He has a blanket (III. 4. 64).*

[38] yokefellow   *partner*

equity   *English law has courts of equity as well as courts of law.*

[39] Bench   *take your seat on the judge's bench*

o'th'commission   *sworn in as a justice*

[42–5] Sleepest . . . harm   *This seems to be a version of what has come down to us as the nursery-rhyme 'Little Boy Blue'. The obvious inference is that if we are to 'deal justly' with Goneril and Regan, we should note that the vigilance of Lear (the shepherd) could have stopped his daughters (the sheep) from having the kingdom (straying into the corn).*

[44] minikin   *pretty little*

[46] Purr . . . gray   *Either Edgar makes a purring noise, or Purr is the name of the cat. Cats were often thought to be the familiar spirits of witches.*

[52] Cry you mercy   *excuse me*

joint-stool   *a 'joined' stool, made by a carpenter, as opposed to one roughly knocked together*

[53] warped   *distorted*

[54] What store . . . on   *what stuff her heart is made of (?)*

[56] justicer   *judge*

[61] mar my counterfeiting   *spoil my acting*

[64] Avaunt   *off with you*

for two white herring. Croak not, black angel; I have
no food for thee.

KENT How do you, sir? Stand you not so amazed.
Will you lie down and rest upon the cushions?

LEAR I'll see their trial first. Bring in their evidence.
[*To* EDGAR] Thou robéd man of justice, take thy
place;
[*To the* FOOL] And thou, his yokefellow of equity,
Bench by his side. [*To* KENT] You are o'th'
commission;
Sit you too.   40

EDGAR Let us deal justly.
    Sleepest or wakest thou, jolly shepherd?
      Thy sheep be in the corn;
    And for one blast of thy minikin mouth
      Thy sheep shall take no harm.
Purr the cat is gray.

LEAR Arraign her first; 'tis Goneril. I here take my
oath before this honourable assembly, she kicked the
poor king, her father.

FOOL Come hither, mistress. Is your name Goneril?   50

LEAR She cannot deny it.

FOOL Cry you mercy, I took you for a joint-stool.

LEAR And here's another, whose warped looks
    proclaim
What store her heart is made on. Stop her there!
Arms, arms, sword, fire! Corruption in the place!
False justicer, why hast thou let her 'scape?

EDGAR Bless thy five wits!

KENT O pity! Sir, where is the patience now
That you so oft have boasted to retain?

EDGAR [*Aside*] My tears begin to take his part so much   60
They mar my counterfeiting.

LEAR The little dogs and all,
Tray, Blanche, and Sweetheart; see, they bark at me.

EDGAR Tom will throw his head at them. Avaunt, you
curs!

[66] or . . . or   *either . . . or*

[69] brach   *bitch*
     lym   *bloodhound*
[70] bobtail . . . trundle-tail   *cur with tail cut short or left drooping*

[73] hatch   *lower half of stable-type door*
[74–5] march . . . towns   *i.e. where there would be more profit for a beggar*
[75] thy horn is dry   *drinking horn is empty*
[76] anatomise   *dissect*
[77] breeds about   *grows around*
[77–8] cause . . . makes   *natural reason (as opposed to divine) for the existence of*
[79] entertain   *engage*
[81] Persian   *i.e. of exotic splendour*

[83–4] draw the curtains   *Lear imagines he is within a four-poster curtained bed.*
[84] go to supper i' th' morning   *He realises they have not eaten.*
[85] And I'll . . . noon   *These are the Fool's last words in the play.*

[89] upon   *against*
[90] litter   *a portable bed, perhaps curtained, to be carried like a stretcher*
[91] drive   *head*

Be thy mouth or black or white,
Tooth that poisons if it bite;
Mastiff, greyhound, mongrel grim,
Hound or spaniel, brach or lym,
Or bobtail tyke or trundle-tail,   70
Tom will make him weep and wail;
For, with throwing thus my head,
Dogs leaped the hatch, and all are fled.
Do, de, de, de. Sessa! Come, march to wakes and
fairs and market towns. Poor Tom, thy horn is dry.

LEAR Then let them anatomise Regan; see what
breeds about her heart. Is there any cause in nature
that makes these hard hearts? [*To* EDGAR] You, sir,
I entertain for one of my hundred; only I do not like
the fashion of your garments. You will say they are   80
Persian; but let them be changed.

KENT Now, good my lord, lie here and rest awhile.

LEAR Make no noise, make no noise; draw the curtains. So, so; we'll go to supper i'th'morning.

FOOL And I'll go to bed at noon.

Enter GLOUCESTER

GLOUCESTER Come hither, friend. Where is the King
my master?

KENT Here, sir, but trouble him not, his wits are
gone.

GLOUCESTER Good friend, I prithee take him in thy
arms.
I have o'erheard a plot of death upon him.
There is a litter ready; lay him in't,   90
And drive toward Dover, friend, where thou shalt
meet
Both welcome and protection. Take up thy master;
If thou should'st dally half an hour, his life,
With thine, and all that offer to defend him,
Stand in assuréd loss. Take up, take up,

165

[96–7] to some . . . conduct   *lead you quickly to where you can get supplies*

[98] balmed . . . sinews   *soothed your shattered nerves*

[100] Stand . . . cure   *will be hard to cure*

[102–3] *When our superiors suffer in the way we do, we don't feel the enmity of fortune so personally.*

[104–5] *It is the solitary sufferer who suffers most, excluded from the care-free life and happy scenes enjoyed by others.*

[106] sufference   *suffering*

[107] bearing   *endurance (of misery)*

[108] portable   *bearable*

[111] Mark . . . noises   *attend to what's going on in high places (?)*

[111–13] thyself . . . reconciles thee   *reveal yourself when false beliefs, whose misconceptions are a stain on you, change, proving you just, and reconciling you to your father*

[114] What . . . more   *whatever else happens*

safe . . . King   *may the King escape safely*

[115] Lurk   *hide*

ACT THREE, scene 7

The cruelty which the evil party in the play are capable of is shown at its fullest extent when Cornwall, with the encouragement of Goneril and the assistance of Regan, puts out Gloucester's eyes with his own hands.

[1] Post   *travel quickly by horse*

[2] letter   *the letter stolen by Edmund from Gloucester*

And follow me, that will to some provision
Give thee quick conduct.

KENT   Oppresséd nature sleeps.
This rest might yet have balmed thy broken
    sinews,
Which, if convenience will not allow,
Stand in hard cure. [*To the* FOOL] Come, help to   100
    bear thy master;
Thou must not stay behind.

GLOUCESTER   Come, come, away!
        [*Exeunt* GLOUCESTER, KENT, *and the* FOOL,
                                carrying LEAR

EDGAR When we our betters see bearing our woes,
We scarcely think our miseries our foes.
Who alone suffers, suffers most i'th' mind,
Leaving free things and happy shows behind.
But then the mind much sufferance doth o'erskip
When grief hath mates, and bearing fellowship.
How light and portable my pain seems now,
When that which makes me bend makes the King
    bow.
He childed as I fathered! Tom, away!   110
Mark the high noises, and thyself bewray
When false opinion, whose wrong thoughts defile
    thee,
In thy just proof repeals and reconciles thee.
What will hap more tonight, safe 'scape the King!
Lurk, lurk.   [*Exit*

Scene 7. *Enter* CORNWALL, REGAN, GONERIL, EDMUND
    and SERVANTS

CORNWALL [*To* GONERIL] Post speedily to my lord
    your husband; show him this letter. The army of
    France is landed. Seek out the traitor Gloucester.
                        [*Exeunt some of the* SERVANTS

[7] our sister *Goneril*

[10] festinate preparation *speedy preparation for war*
[11-12] posts ... intelligent *mounted messengers shall be fast and carry full information*
[13] Lord of Gloucester *In Cornwall's eyes, Edmund has already succeeded his father. When Oswald enters, he refers, of course, to the father.*

[16] his *Lear's*
[17] questrists *seekers*
[18] the lord's dependants *Gloucester's men*

[23] Pinion *bind*

[24] pass ... life *condemn him to death*
[25] form *formalities*
[25-6] power ... wrath *limited power shall not stand in the way of our wrath*
[27] control *hold back*

[29] corky *dry with age, like a cork*

REGAN Hang him instantly.

GONERIL Pluck out his eyes.

CORNWALL Leave him to my displeasure. Edmund,
keep you our sister company. The revenges we are
bound to take upon your traitorous father are not
fit for your beholding. Advise the Duke, where you
are going, to a most festinate preparation: we are   10
bound to the like. Our posts shall be swift and
intelligent betwixt us. Farewell, dear sister; farewell,
my Lord of Gloucester.

Enter OSWALD

How now? Where's the King?

OSWALD My Lord of Gloucester hath conveyed him
    hence.
Some five or six and thirty of his knights,
Hot questrists after him, met him at gate,
Who, with some other of the lord's dependants,
Are gone with him toward Dover, where they
    boast
To have well-arméd friends.

CORNWALL   Get horses for your mistress.   20

GONERIL Farewell, sweet lord, and sister.

CORNWALL Edmund, farewell.

                [*Exeunt* GONERIL, EDMUND *and* OSWALD
                    Go seek the traitor Gloucester.
Pinion him like a thief, bring him before us.
                        [*Exeunt other* SERVANTS
Though well we may not pass upon his life
Without the form of justice, yet our power
Shall do a court'sy to our wrath, which men
May blame, but not control.

Enter SERVANTS, *with* GLOUCESTER *prisoner*
                    Who's there? The traitor?

REGAN Ingrateful fox! 'tis he.

CORNWALL Bind fast his corky arms.

[plucks his beard] (*an extreme insult*)

[37] Naughty   *wicked*

[39] quicken   *come to life*

[40] hospitable favours   *either 'kindness as a host' or 'the features (i.e. face) of your host'*

[41] ruffle   *treat violently*

[42] late   *recently*

[43] Be simple-answered   *answer directly, without evasion*

[44] confederacy   *unlawful alliance*

[45] footed   *landed*

[45–6] To . . . king   *Regan completes the question begun by Cornwall.*

[47] guessingly set down   *written from speculation*

[51] charged at peril   *ordered under threat of punishment*

GLOUCESTER What means your Graces? Good my   30
   friends, consider
  You are my guests. Do me no foul play, friends.
CORNWALL Bind him, I say.

                        [SERVANTS *bind him*
REGAN   Hard, hard. O filthy traitor!
GLOUCESTER Unmerciful lady as you are, I'm none.
CORNWALL To this chair bind him. Villain, thou
   shalt find—

                      [REGAN *plucks his beard*
GLOUCESTER By the kind gods, 'tis most ignobly done
  To pluck me by the beard.
REGAN So white, and such a traitor?
GLOUCESTER   Naughty lady,
  These hairs which thou dost ravish from my chin
  Will quicken and accuse thee. I am your host.
  With robbers' hands my hospitable favours   40
  You should not ruffle thus. What will you do?
CORNWALL Come, sir. What letters had you late
   from France?
REGAN Be simple-answered, for we know the truth.
CORNWALL And what confederacy have you with the
   traitors
  Late footed in the kingdom—
REGAN   —To whose hands
  You have sent the lunatic king? Speak.
GLOUCESTER I have a letter, guessingly set down,
  Which came from one that's of a neutral heart,
  And not from one opposed.
CORNWALL   Cunning.
REGAN   And false.
CORNWALL Where hast thou sent the King?
GLOUCESTER   To Dover.   50
REGAN Wherefore to Dover? Wast thou not charged
   at peril—
CORNWALL Wherefore to Dover? Let him answer
   that.

[53] tied ... course *The image is from bear-baiting, a 'sport' very popular in the theatre-district of the Bankside where this play was originally performed. A bear would be chained to a post and dogs would be set on to attack him, a certain number at each 'course'.*

[57] anointed *made sacred by holy oil at the sacrament of the coronation ceremony*

rash boarish fangs *stick her nails as savagely as if they were the tusks of the wild boar*

[59] buoyed *risen*

[60] stelléd fires *stars*

[61] holp *helped*

[62] dern *dark and dreary*

[64] All ... subscribe *otherwise, you countenance all cruelty (i.e. if you don't pity even wolves and give them shelter, you are assenting to cruelty)*

[65] wingéd Vengeance *Vengeance is personified as an angel of wrath.*

[68] will think *hopes*

live ... old *i.e. escape divine wrath. But the servant who comes to his help does not live to be old.*

[70] mock another *make the other look silly (not matching)*

[74] bid you hold *tell you to stop*

[75-6] If you ... shake it *i.e. if you were a man, I would do to you what you did to Gloucester*

[76] What ... mean? *(strongly emphasised) what on earth do you have in mind?*

[77] My villain *my serf (said with contempt and indignation)*

[78] take ... anger *take your chance in a contest of anger*

GLOUCESTER I am tied to th' stake, and I must stand
    the course.
REGAN Wherefore to Dover?
GLOUCESTER Because I would not see thy cruel nails
    Pluck out his poor old eyes, nor thy fierce sister
    In his anointed flesh rash boarish fangs.
    The sea, with such a storm as his bare head
    In hell-black night endured, would have buoyed up,
    And quenched the stelléd fires;   60
    Yet, poor old heart, he holp the heavens to rain.
    If wolves had at thy gate howled that dern time,
    Thou should'st have said 'Good porter, turn the
        key;
    All cruels else subscribe.' But I shall see
    The wingéd Vengeance overtake such children.
CORNWALL See 't shalt thou never. Fellows, hold
    the chair.
    Upon these eyes of thine I'll set my foot.
GLOUCESTER He that will think to live till he be old,
    Give me some help! – O cruel! O you gods!
REGAN One side will mock another. Th'other too!   70
CORNWALL If you see vengeance—
FIRST SERVANT   Hold your hand, my lord!
    I have served you ever since I was a child,
    But better service have I never done you
    Than now to bid you hold.
REGAN   How now, you dog?
FIRST SERVANT If you did wear a beard upon your
    chin,
    I'd shake it on this quarrel. What do you mean?
CORNWALL My villain?   [*He draws his sword*
FIRST SERVANT [*Drawing his sword*] Nay, then, come
    on, and take the chance of anger.

        They fight; CORNWALL *is wounded*

REGAN [*To another* SERVANT] Give me thy sword. A
    peasant stand up thus?

[81] mischief on him *injury to him*
[Dies] *The first of many deaths in the play; a man of courage and honesty murdered by Regan.*

[85] sparks of nature *fire of family feeling*
[86] quit *requite, avenge*

[88] overture *disclosure*

[90] abused *wrongfully treated*
[91] forgive . . . him *In all his pain and shock, Gloucester's first thought is for Edgar, and regret for the wrong he has done him.*

[93] How look you? *How are you?*

[95] this slave *the dead servant*
[96] apace *fast*

[100] old course *usual way (as against a divinely-sent vengeance)*

[102] the bedlam *Poor Tom*

[104] Allows . . . anything *makes him agreeable to anything you suggest*

174

She takes a sword and runs at him behind

FIRST SERVANT O, I am slain! My lord, you have   80
    one eye left
  To see some mischief on him. O!   [*Dies*

CORNWALL Lest it see more, prevent it. Out, vile
    jelly!
  Where is thy lustre now?

GLOUCESTER All dark and comfortless! Where's my
    son Edmund?
  Edmund, enkindle all the sparks of nature
  To quit this horrid act.

REGAN   Out, treacherous villain!
  Thou call'st on him that hates thee. It was he
  That made the overture of thy treasons to us,
  Who is too good to pity thee.

GLOUCESTER O, my follies! Then Edgar was abused.   90
  Kind gods, forgive me that, and prosper him!

REGAN Go thrust him out at gates, and let him smell
  His way to Dover.

             [*Exit a* SERVANT *with* GLOUCESTER
             How is't, my lord? How look you?

CORNWALL I have received a hurt. Follow me, lady.
  Turn out that eyeless villain. Throw this slave
  Upon the dunghill. Regan, I bleed apace.
  Untimely comes this hurt. Give me your arm.
            [*Exeunt* CORNWALL *and* REGAN

SECOND SERVANT I'll never care what wickedness I
    do,
  If this man come to good.

THIRD SERVANT   If she live long,
  And in the end meet the old course of death,   100
  Women will all turn monsters.

SECOND SERVANT Let's follow the old earl, and get
    the bedlam
  To lead him where he would; his roguish madness
  Allows itself to anything.

[105] **flax** *Flax was used as a lint to make plasters.*

THIRD SERVANT Go thou; I'll fetch some flax and
whites of eggs
To apply to his bleeding face. Now heaven help
him!

[*Exeunt*

ACT FOUR, scene 1

*Edgar meets his blinded father but does not reveal his identity.
The scene is full of thoughts about the drawbacks of different
human conditions. Both Edgar and Gloucester seem to conclude
that to have reached the bottom may be better than falling.*

[1] known . . . contemned   *to know that one is despised*
[3] dejected   *cast down*
[4] Stands . . . esperance   *is always in the position of hoping*
[6] worst . . . laughter   *the worst situation can only change to a
happier one*
[7] unsubstantial   *(1) lacking body (2) lacking money*
[9] Owes nothing to   *If he had been beggared by a man of
substance, he would still owe him money, and live in fear. He has
nothing more to fear from the elements.*

[10] poorly eyed   *The text is corrupt; this is one of a number of
suggested readings.*
[11–12] But that . . . age   *if it were not for the fact that the
unaccountable ups-and-downs of fortune make us hate the world,
we should not be willing to grow old. This is a strange thought, but
the idea that the world is an enemy to whom one is too proud to surrender by shortening one's life is important in the development of
Edgar's role.*

[16] comforts   *efforts to comfort me*
[17] hurt   *as assisting an alleged traitor*

[19] I stumbled . . . saw   *I made mistakes when I had my vision*
[20–21] Our means . . . commodities   *property and possessions
give us a false sense of security, and the absence of these things may
be of advantage to us*
[22] abuséd   *deceived*

ACT FOUR

Scene 1. *Enter* EDGAR

EDGAR Yet better thus, and known to be contemned,
  Than still contemned and flattered. To be worst,
  The lowest and most dejected thing of Fortune,
  Stands still in esperance, lives not in fear.
  The lamentable change is from the best;
  The worst returns to laughter. Welcome, then,
  Thou unsubstantial air that I embrace:
  The wretch that thou hast blown unto the worst
  Owes nothing to thy blasts.

  Enter GLOUCESTER, *led by an* OLD MAN

                     But who comes here?
  My father, poorly eyed! World, world, O world!   10
  But that thy strange mutations make us hate thee,
  Life would not yield to age.
OLD MAN   O my good lord,
  I have been your tenant, and your father's tenant,
  These fourscore years.
GLOUCESTER Away, get thee away! Good friend, be
    gone.
  Thy comforts can do me no good at all;
  Thee they may hurt.
OLD MAN   You cannot see your way.
GLOUCESTER I have no way, and therefore want no
    eyes;
  I stumbled when I saw. Full oft 'tis seen
  Our means secure us, and our mere defects   20
  Prove our commodities. O dear son Edgar,
  The food of thy abuséd father's wrath!
  Might I but live to see thee in my touch,
  I'd say I had eyes again.
OLD MAN   How now? Who's there?

[27-8] **the worst . . . worst** *i.e. things may go on getting worse so long as we have life and consciousness*

[31] **reason** *mental power*

[36-7] **As flies . . . sport** *After 'I have heard more since', Gloucester pauses to ask what reason there can be in what he and Edgar have suffered. His answer is the bitter comment that the gods have no more love and care for us than boys have for the flies they carelessly kill. He may be excused his bitterness, but he perhaps forgets his own complicity in Edgar's misfortunes.*

[36] **wanton boys** *boys playing irresponsibly*

[37] **How . . . be** *Edgar is bewildered at his father's injuries, at his sudden friendliness towards him, and at his attack on the gods.*

[38-9] **Bad . . . others** *Edgar hates himself for having to continue his clowning impersonation in the present situation.*

[43] **ancient** *of long standing (and hence old-fashioned)*

[46] **the time's plague** *characteristic disease of the times*

[47] **or . . . pleasure** *He feels he no longer has the right to give orders.*

[48] **the rest** *everything else*

[49] **'parel** *apparel, clothing*

EDGAR [*Aside*] O gods! Who is't can say 'I am at the
    worst'?
  I am worse than e'er I was.

OLD MAN   'Tis poor mad Tom.

EDGAR [*Aside*] And worse I may be yet; the worst
    is not
  So long as we can say 'This is the worst'.

OLD MAN Fellow, where goest?

GLOUCESTER   Is it a beggar-man?

OLD MAN Madman and beggar too.   30

GLOUCESTER He has some reason, else he could not
    beg.
  I' th' last night's storm I such a fellow saw,
  Which made me think a man a worm. My son
  Came then into my mind, and yet my mind
  Was then scarce friends with him. I have heard
    more since.
  As flies to wanton boys are we to th' gods;
  They kill us for their sport.

EDGAR [*Aside*]   How should this be?
  Bad is the trade that must play fool to sorrow,
  Angering itself and others. – Bless thee, master!

GLOUCESTER Is that the naked fellow?

OLD MAN   Ay, my lord.   40

GLOUCESTER Then prithee get thee gone. If, for my
    sake,
  Thou wilt o'ertake us hence a mile or twain
  I' th' way toward Dover, do it for ancient love;
  And bring some covering for this naked soul
  Which I'll entreat to lead me.

OLD MAN   Alack, sir, he is mad!

GLOUCESTER 'Tis the time's plague when madmen
    lead the blind.
  Do as I bid thee; or rather do thy pleasure.
  Above the rest, be gone.

OLD MAN I'll bring him the best 'parel that I have,
  Come on't what will.   [*Exit*

[51] daub it *plaster it on. He cannot keep up the impersonation.*

[57] **Bless thee** *God protect thee*

[59–61] Obidicut . . . Flibbertigibbet *These names are all versions of those found by Shakespeare in Harsnett's book.*

[61] mopping and mowing *making faces*

[65] humbled to all strokes *abased so much that he accepts all misfortunes*
[66] happier *i.e. by having a companion in misfortune*
　　　deal so still *always see that miseries are shared out*
[67] superfluous . . . man *man who has too much and is fed by his pleasures*
[68] slaves your ordinance *treats your law contemptuously*
[68–9] will not see . . . feel *will not realise the existence of misery because he doesn't feel it*
[70] distribution *sharing out*
[71] each . . . enough *Gloucester is really talking about the sharing out of misery; but he turns here to the obvious corollary, that wealth should be shared out too.*
[74] Looks fearfully *Even the cliff is frightened to look down.*
　　　confinéd *hemmed in by the cliffs*
[76] repair *remedy*

GLOUCESTER   Sirrah, naked fellow!   50

EDGAR Poor Tom's a-cold. [*Aside*] I cannot daub it
     further.

GLOUCESTER Come hither, fellow.

EDGAR [*Aside*] And yet I must. Bless thy sweet eyes,
     they bleed!

GLOUCESTER Know'st thou the way to Dover?

EDGAR Both stile and gate, horseway and footpath.
     Poor Tom hath been scared out of his good wits.
     Bless thee, good man's son, from the foul fiend!
     Five fiends have been in poor Tom at once: as
     Obidicut, of lust; Hobbididence, prince of dumb-
     ness; Mahu, of stealing; Modo, of murder;   60
     Flibbertigibbet, of mopping and mowing, who since
     possesses chambermaids and waiting-women. So,
     bless thee, master!

GLOUCESTER Here, take this purse, thou whom the
     heavens' plagues
     Have humbled to all strokes. That I am wretched
     Makes thee the happier. Heavens, deal so still!
     Let the superfluous and lust-dieted man,
     That slaves your ordinance, that will not see
     Because he does not feel, feel your power quickly;
     So distribution should undo excess,   70
     And each man have enough. Dost thou know
     Dover?

EDGAR Ay, master.

GLOUCESTER There is a cliff, whose high and bending
     head
     Looks fearfully in the confinéd deep.
     Bring me but to the very brim of it,
     And I'll repair the misery thou dost bear
     With something rich about me. From that place
     I shall no leading need.

EDGAR   Give me thy arm;
     Poor Tom shall lead thee.   [*Exeunt*

ACT FOUR, scene 2

Albany dissociates himself from Goneril and the anti-Lear party. With the news of Cornwall's death, both sisters are without their husbands' help, and Edmund comes into a position of new importance.

[1] Welcome   *She welcomes him as they arrive together.*

[8] sot   *fool*
[9] wrong side out   *in calling Gloucester a traitor and Edmund loyal*

[12] cowish   *cowardly*
[13] undertake   *initiate an action*
    feel   *show feeling or recognition of*
[14] wishes   *concerning our love*
    way   *journey*
[15] prove effects   *become realities*
[16] musters   *gathering of troops*
    powers   *forces*
[17] distaff   *stick used in spinning wool; symbol of the female role*

[21] A mistress's command   *i.e. to come as her lover*

Scene 2. *Enter* GONERIL *and* EDMUND

GONERIL Welcome, my lord. I marvel our mild
    husband
  Not met us on the way.

Enter OSWALD

              Now, where's your master?
OSWALD Madam, within; but never man so changed.
  I told him of the army that was landed;
  He smiled at it. I told him you were coming;
  His answer was, 'The worse'. Of Gloucester's
    treachery
  And of the loyal service of his son
  When I informed him, then he called me sot
  And told me I had turned the wrong side out.
  What most he should dislike seems pleasant to   10
    him;
  What like, offensive.
GONERIL [*To* EDMUND] Then shall you go no further.
  It is the cowish terror of his spirit,
  That dares not undertake. He'll not feel wrongs
  Which tie him to an answer. Our wishes on the
    way
  May prove effects. Back, Edmund, to my brother;
  Hasten his musters and conduct his powers.
  I must change names at home and give the distaff
  Into my husband's hands. This trusty servant
  Shall pass between us; ere long you are like to
    hear
  (If you dare venture in your own behalf)   20
  A mistress's command. Wear this [*Giving a
    favour*]. Spare speech.
  Decline your head. This kiss, if it durst speak,

[23] stretch . . . up (*1*) *exhilarate you* (*2*) *sexually excite you*

[25] death *In the mind, as in common language, death often fuses with the fulfilment of love.*

[29] I . . . whistling *The proverb is 'It's a poor dog that's not worth whistling'; Goneril means that in not coming to meet her, Albany shows how little he now cares for her.*

[31] fear *distrust*
 disposition *character*
[32] contemns *despises*
 its origin *i.e. Lear*
[33] bordered certain *contained within definite limits*
[34–5] sliver . . . sap *The image is of a branch torn from the tree whose sap gives it nourishment.*
[36] deadly use *burned in the fire*
[37] text is foolish *you have chosen a foolish subject for your sermon*
[39] Filths . . . themselves *everything tastes like filth to the filthy*
[42] head-lugged *being dragged by a chain round its neck*

[43] madded *driven mad*

[46] visible spirits *Albany hopes to see in the actions of men evidence that God is shaping human history. See ll. 78–80.*
[48–50] It will . . . deep *The ultimate condition of men who have neither reason nor religion in them will be that they will hunt and eat each other as savage fish of the deep sea do.*

Would stretch thy spirits up into the air.
Conceive, and fare thee well.

EDMUND Yours in the ranks of death!

GONERIL   My most dear Gloucester!
                              [*Exit* EDMUND

O, the difference of man and man!
To thee a woman's services are due;
A fool usurps my bed.

OSWALD   Madam, here comes my lord. [*Exit*

Enter ALBANY

GONERIL I have been worth the whistling.

ALBANY   O Goneril,
You are not worth the dust which the rude wind   30
Blows in your face! I fear your disposition.
That nature which contemns its origin
Cannot be bordered certain in itself.
She that herself will sliver and disbranch
From her material sap, perforce must wither
And come to deadly use.

GONERIL No more! The text is foolish.

ALBANY Wisdom and goodness to the vile seem vile;
Filths savour but themselves. What have you done?
Tigers, not daughters, what have you performed?   40
A father, and a gracious agéd man,
Whose reverence even the head-lugged bear would
    lick,
Most barbarous, most degenerate, have you
    madded.
Could my good brother suffer you to do it?
A man, a prince, by him so benefited!
If that the heavens do not their visible spirits
Send quickly down to tame these vile offences,
It will come
Humanity must perforce prey on itself
Like monsters of the deep.

[50] Milk-livered (*milk instead of blood*) *cowardly*

[51] for *made to receive*

[53] honour . . . suffering *the occasion for retaliation from the occasion for putting up with something*

[54–5] Fools . . . mischief *only fools waste compassion on wrongdoers who have been stopped from committing wrongs by a pre-emptive punishment.* (*The common specious justification for aggression: that you are preventing aggression from the other side.*)

[56] noiseless *without the noise of war-preparation*

[57] helm *helmet*

thy . . . threat *begins to threaten your realm*

[58] a moral fool *one foolish enough to consider everything in moral terms*

[60] Proper . . . fiend *deformity, which is suited to the devil, does not seem in him . . .*

[62] changéd *transformed*

self-covered *concealing the true self* (?)

[63] Bemonster . . . feature *don't let your beastliness appear in your face*

Were't my fitness *if it were proper for me*

[64] blood *passion*

[65] apt *ready*

[66–7] Howe'er . . . shield thee *Even though you are a devil, you still have the appearance of a woman, and that protects you from my fury*

[68] Marry *by the Virgin Mary*

your manhood! *who are you to talk of what is fit for man or woman?*

mew! *The text is uncertain; possibly Goneril makes a noise like a cat.*

[73] bred *brought up*

thrilled with remorse *excited by compassion*

[75] To *against*

[76] amongst them felled *between them they felled*

GONERIL   Milk-livered man!   50
  That bear'st a cheek for blows, a head for wrongs;
  Who hast not in thy brows an eye discerning
  Thine honour from thy suffering; that not know'st
  Fools do those villains pity who are punished
  Ere they have done their mischief. Where's thy
    drum?
  France spreads his banners in our noiseless land,
  With pluméd helm thy state begins to threat,
  Whilst thou, a moral fool, sits still and cries
  'Alack, why does he so?'
ALBANY   See thyself, devil!
  Proper deformity shows not in the fiend   60
  So horrid as in woman.
GONERIL   O vain fool!
ALBANY Thou changéd and self-covered thing, for
    shame
  Bemonster not thy feature! Were't my fitness
  To let these hands obey my blood,
  They are apt enough to dislocate and tear
  Thy flesh and bones. Howe'er thou art a fiend,
  A woman's shape doth shield thee.
GONERIL Marry, your manhood! mew!

Enter a MESSENGER

ALBANY What news?
MESSENGER O, my good lord, the Duke of Cornwall's   70
    dead,
  Slain by his servant, going to put out
  The other eye of Gloucester.
ALBANY   Gloucester's eyes!
MESSENGER A servant that he bred, thrilled with
    remorse,
  Opposed against the act, bending his sword
  To his great master; who, thereat enraged,
  Flew on him, and amongst them felled him dead;

[78] plucked . . . after   *drawn him after the servant to death*

[79] justicers   *heavenly judges*
    nether   *belonging to this lower world*
[80] venge   *avenge*

[85] all . . . fancy   *all that my fantasy has built up (as regards herself and Edmund)*
[85–6] pluck . . . life   *pull down to the level of my present hateful life*
[87] tart   *bitter*

[90] back   *on his way back*

But not without that harmful stroke which since
Hath plucked him after.

ALBANY   This shows you are above,
You justicers, that these our nether crimes
So speedily can venge! But, O poor Gloucester!   80
Lost he his other eye?

MESSENGER   Both, both, my lord.
This letter, madam, craves a speedy answer;
'Tis from your sister.

GONERIL [*Aside*]   One way I like this well;
But being widow, and my Gloucester with her,
May all the building in my fancy pluck
Upon my hateful life. Another way
The news is not so tart. – I'll read, and answer.
                                                    [*Exit*

ALBANY Where was his son when they did take his
    eyes?

MESSENGER Come with my lady hither.

ALBANY   He is not here.

MESSENGER No, my good lord; I met him back   90
    again.

ALBANY Knows he the wickedness?

MESSENGER Ay, my good lord; 'twas he informed
    against him,
And quit the house on purpose, that their
    punishment
Might have the freer course.

ALBANY   Gloucester, I live
To thank thee for the love thou show'dst the
    King,
And to revenge thine eyes. Come hither, friend;
Tell me what more thou know'st.
                                                    [*Exeunt*

ACT FOUR, scene 3

*We are now near Dover. Cordelia's reactions to Lear's suffer-
ings are described. (Father and daughter have not met.) This
scene is cut in the Folio text.*

[1–7] To have had the French king fighting on English soil might
have risked losing the sympathy of Shakespeare's audience for Cordelia and her cause.

[3] imperfect *unfinished*

[10–11] pierce . . . grief *affect her so keenly that she showed her
grief openly*

[13] trilled *flowed*

[15] passion, who *emotions, which*

[17–18] patience . . . goodliest *self-control and grief were com-
petitors, and each made her look beautiful*

[20] like . . . way *similar but more beautiful (?)*
smilets *little smiles*

[25] so become it *make it appear so lovely*

[26] heaved *brought with difficulty*

Scene 3. *Enter* KENT *and a* GENTLEMAN

KENT Why the King of France is so suddenly gone
back know you no reason?

GENTLEMAN Something he left imperfect in the state,
which since his coming forth is thought of, which
imports to the kingdom so much fear and danger
that his personal return was most required and
necessary.

KENT Who hath he left behind him general?

GENTLEMAN The Marshal of France, Monsieur La Far.

KENT Did your letters pierce the queen to any   10
demonstration of grief?

GENTLEMAN Ay, sir; she took them, read them in my
presence,
And now and then an ample tear trilled down
Her delicate cheek. It seemed she was a queen
Over her passion, who, most rebel-like,
Sought to be king o'er her.

KENT   O, then it moved her.

GENTLEMAN Not to a rage; patience and sorrow
strove
Who should express her goodliest. You have seen
Sunshine and rain at once; her smiles and tears
Were like a better way; those happy smilets   20
That played on her ripe lip seemed not to know
What guests were in her eyes, which parted thence
As pearls from diamonds dropped. In brief,
Sorrow would be a rarity most beloved
If all could so become it.

KENT   Made she no verbal question?

GENTLEMAN Faith, once or twice she heaved the
name of 'father'
Pantingly forth, as if it pressed her heart;
Cried 'Sisters, sisters! Shame of ladies! Sisters!
Kent! father! sisters! What, i'th' storm? i'th' night?

[32] **That . . . moistened**   *that her outcry moistened. (The text is uncertain at this point.)*

[34] **conditions**   *characters*
[35] **one . . . make**   *the same man and wife*
[36] **issues**   *children*

[40] **tune**   *disposition*

[43] **sovereign**   *over-mastering*
     elbows him   *i.e. keeps him back by blows with the elbow*
[44] **stripped her**   *tore her away*

[45] **foreign casualties**   *hazards abroad*

[50] **'Tis so**   *it is a fact that*

[52] **dear cause**   *important matter of concern. Kent's great cause is the reconciliation of Lear and Cordelia; he will reveal himself to Lear only when the work is done.*

Let pity not believe it!' There she shook   30
The holy water from her heavenly eyes
That clamour moistened; then away she started
To deal with grief alone.

KENT   It is the stars.
The stars above us, govern our conditions;
Else one self mate and make could not beget
Such different issues. You spoke not with her
    since?

GENTLEMAN No.

KENT Was this before the King returned?

GENTLEMAN   No, since.

KENT Well, sir, the poor distresséd Lear's i'th' town,
Who sometime, in his better tune, remembers   40
What we are come about, and by no means
Will yield to see his daughter.

GENTLEMAN   Why, good sir?

KENT A sovereign shame so elbows him: his own
    unkindness,
That stripped her from his benediction, turned
    her
To foreign casualties, gave her dear rights
To his dog-hearted daughters – these things sting
His mind so venomously that burning shame
Detains him from Cordelia.

GENTLEMAN   Alack, poor gentleman!

KENT Of Albany's and Cornwall's powers you heard
    not?

GENTLEMAN 'Tis so, they are afoot.   50

KENT Well, sir, I'll bring you to our master Lear
And leave you to attend him. Some dear cause
Will in concealment wrap me up awhile;
When I am known aright, you shall not grieve
Lending me this acquaintance. I pray you go
Along with me.

                        [*Exeunt*

ACT FOUR, scene 4

Cordelia reappears on the stage after her long absence (since I. I). She is at the head of the French army, but her main concern is for her crazed father.

[3] fumiter   *fumitory, a bitter herb*
     furrow-weeds   *weeds growing in the furrows of ploughed land*
[4] hardocks   (*not identified*)
     hemlock   *common poisonous weed with white flower*
     cuckoo-flowers   *cuckoo-pint or wake robin: poisonous*
[5] Darnel   *a wild grass*
[6] sustaining corn   *wheat etc., which maintains life*
     century   *troop of a hundred soldiers*
[7] high-grown field   *This indication that it is now late summer raises the question of what season the rest of the play is imagined in. The weather is more notable than the seasons in King Lear, and the storm, with its rain, wind, thunder, and cold, could belong to any season.*
[8–9] What can . . . restoring   *what can science do to restore*
[10] outward worth   *material possessions*
[13] That . . . provoke   *to bring about repose*
[14] simples   *herbs*
     operative   *efficacious*
[17] Spring with my tears   *come forth, watered by my tears*
     aidant   *beneficial*
[20] wants . . . lead it   *lacks the rationality to govern it*

[26] importuned   *importunate, demanding*
[27] blown   *puffed up*
     our arms incite   *urge our army on*

Scene 4. *Enter, with drum and colours,* CORDELIA,
DOCTOR *and* SOLDIERS

CORDELIA Alack, 'tis he! Why, he was met even now
As mad as the vexed sea, singing aloud,
Crowned with rank fumiter and furrow-weeds,
With hardocks, hemlock, nettles, cuckoo-flowers,
Darnel, and all the idle weeds that grow
In our sustaining corn. A century send forth;
Search every acre in the high-grown field,
And bring him to our eye. [*Exit an* OFFICER] What
  can man's wisdom
In the restoring his bereavéd sense?
He that helps him take all my outward worth.   10
DOCTOR There is means, madam.
Our foster-nurse of nature is repose,
The which he lacks. That to provoke in him
Are many simples operative, whose power
Will close the eye of anguish.
CORDELIA   All blest secrets,
All you unpublished virtues of the earth,
Spring with my tears! Be aidant and remediate
In the good man's distress! – Seek, seek for him,
Lest his ungoverned rage dissolve the life
That wants the means to lead it.

Enter MESSENGER

MESSENGER   News, madam!   20
The British powers are marching hitherward.
CORDELIA 'Tis known before; our preparation stands
In expectation of them. O dear father,
It is thy business that I go about!
Therefore great France
My mourning and importuned tears hath pitied.
No blown ambition doth our arms incite,

ACT FOUR, scene 5

*The spirit of contention among the rulers of divided England,
which we heard about before in the whispers of dissension
between Cornwall and Albany, breaks out again in the jealousy
between the sisters for the love of Edmund.*

[2] with much ado   *after a great deal of bother*

[6] import   *be the significance of*

[8] is posted   *has ridden out quickly*
    on serious matter   *i.e. he is not to be bothered by letters from
Goneril*

[13] nighted   *darkened*
    descry   *discover*

[18] charged my duty   *laid on me a solemn obligation*

[20] Belike   *perhaps*

But love, dear love, and our aged father's right.⌉
Soon may I hear and see him!

[*Exeunt*

Scene 5. *Enter* REGAN *and* OSWALD

REGAN But are my brother's powers set forth?
OSWALD   Ay, madam.
REGAN Himself in person there?
OSWALD   Madam, with much ado.
  Your sister is the better soldier.
REGAN Lord Edmund spake not with your lord at
    home?
OSWALD No, madam.
REGAN What might import my sister's letter to him?
OSWALD I know not, lady.
REGAN Faith, he is posted hence on serious matter.
  It was great ignorance, Gloucester's eyes being
    out,
  To let him live. Where he arrives he moves   10
  All hearts against us. Edmund, I think, is gone,
  In pity of his misery, to dispatch
  His nighted life; moreover, to descry
  The strength o'th' enemy.
OSWALD I must needs after him, madam, with my
    letter.
REGAN Our troops set forth tomorrow. Stay with us;
  The ways are dangerous.
OSWALD   I may not, madam;
  My lady charged my duty in this business.
REGAN Why should she write to Edmund? Might
    not you
  Transport her purposes by word? Belike,   20
  Some things, I know not what. I'll love thee
    much—
  Let me unseal the letter.

[24] late *lately*
[25] oeillades *amorous glances*
[26] of her bosom *in her confidence*

[29] take this note *take note of this*

[31] convenient *fitting*
[32] gather *infer*
[33] this *a token(?)*

[35] call *recall*

[38] Preferment *promotion*

ACT FOUR, scene 6

In the fields near Dover, Edgar uses a strange stratagem to turn Gloucester from suicide. The two injured fathers, mad Lear and blind Gloucester, come together. Lear's manic patter, conveying a profound and painful assessment of man's life, is one of the most brilliant things Shakespeare does in this play. Edgar continues the work of restoring the balance of good against evil in overcoming Oswald.

[6] By . . . anguish *because of the pain of your eyes*

OSWALD   Madam, I had rather—
REGAN I know your lady does not love her
      husband—
   I am sure of that; and at her late being here
   She gave strange oeillades and most speaking looks
   To noble Edmund. I know you are of her bosom.
OSWALD I, madam?
REGAN I speak in understanding. Y'are; I know't.
   Therefore I do advise you take this note.
   My lord is dead; Edmund and I have talked,   30
   And more convenient is he for my hand
   Than for your lady's. You may gather more.
   If you do find him, pray you give him this;
   And when your mistress hears thus much from
      you,
   I pray desire her call her wisdom to her.
   So fare you well.
   If you do chance to hear of that blind traitor,
   Preferment falls on him that cuts him off.
OSWALD Would I could meet him, madam! I should
      show
   What party I do follow.
REGAN   Fare thee well.   40
                                    [Exeunt

Scene 6. *Enter* GLOUCESTER *and* EDGAR

   GLOUCESTER When shall I come to th' top of that
      same hill?
   EDGAR You do climb up it now. Look how we labour.
   GLOUCESTER Methinks the ground is even.
   EDGAR   Horrible steep.
   Hark, do you hear the sea?
   GLOUCESTER   No, truly.
   EDGAR Why then your other senses grow imperfect
   By your eyes' anguish.

[9] Y're much deceived *It is Edgar's plan throughout this scene to unsettle and bewilder Gloucester by making him uncertain of the evidence of his remaining senses. This is not only to make Gloucester accept his 'fall' from the cliff; it also has the important effect of making the new Gloucester feel he has come through a period of illusion and untruth induced by the devil.*

[11–24] *Edgar, who so wonderfully acted the part of a mad beggar, now does a brilliant impersonation of a man looking over a cliff. In the theatre, it is important that the actor taking Edgar's part makes it clear to the audience that Edgar is making it all up, for those who do not know the story are often led by the superb description to think that this scene does actually take place on a cliff-top, and they are baffled by what follows.*

[13] choughs *('chuffs') big black birds, common on cliffs in the west of Britain and Ireland but no longer in southeast England*

[14] gross *large*

[15] samphire *aromatic herb*

[19] cock *dinghy*

[21] unnumbered idle pebble *innumerable pebbles shifting about like a crowd of people with nothing to do*

[23–4] deficient . . . Topple *dizziness make me topple*

[27] leap upright *make even an upwards jump, let alone forward*

[29–30] Fairies . . . thee *may fairies and gods make the jewel bring good to you*

GLOUCESTER   So may it be indeed.
   Methinks thy voice is altered, and thou speak'st
   In better phrase and matter than thou didst.
EDGAR Y'are much deceived; in nothing am I
      changed
   But in my garments.
GLOUCESTER   Methinks y'are better spoken. 10
EDGAR Come on, sir, here's the place. Stand still.
      How fearful
   And dizzy 'tis to cast one's eyes so low!
   The crows and choughs that wing the midway air
   Show scarce so gross as beetles. Half way down
   Hangs one that gathers samphire – dreadful trade!
   Methinks he seems no bigger than his head.
   The fishermen that walk upon the beach
   Appear like mice; and yon tall anchoring bark
   Diminished to her cock; her cock a buoy
   Almost too small for sight. The murmuring surge, 20
   That on th'unnumbered idle pebble chafes,
   Cannot be heard so high. I'll look no more,
   Lest my brain turn, and the deficient sight
   Topple down headlong.
GLOUCESTER   Set me where you stand.
EDGAR Give me your hand. You are now within a
      foot
   Of th'extreme verge. For all beneath the moon
   Would I not leap upright.
GLOUCESTER   Let go my hand.
   Here, friend, 's another purse, in it a jewel
   Well worth a poor man's taking. Fairies and gods
   Prosper it with thee! Go thou further off.   30
   Bid me farewell, and let me hear thee going.
EDGAR Now fare ye well, good sir.
GLOUCESTER   With all my heart!
EDGAR [Aside] Why I do trifle thus with his despair
   Is done to cure it.
GLOUCESTER   O you mighty gods! [He kneels

[36] patiently *in resignation, not hot anger*
[37–8] fall . . . quarrel with *begin to rebel against*
[38] opposeless *irresistible*
[39] snuff . . . part *the reeking wick left as the candle burns out*

[42–4] conceit . . . theft *i.e. imagination might cause death when the man had no wish to live*

[45] By this . . . past *by this time thinking would have been all over*

[47] pass *die*

[49] gossamer *cobweb filaments floating in the air*

[50] precipitating *falling headlong*

[53] at each *one on top of the other*

[57] bourn *boundary (of the land)*
[58] shrill-gorged *shrill-throated*

This world I do renounce, and in your sights
Shake patiently my great affliction off.
If I could bear it longer, and not fall
To quarrel with your great opposeless wills,
My snuff and loathéd part of nature should
Burn itself out. If Edgar live, O bless him!   40
Now, fellow, fare thee well.

EDGAR   Gone, sir; farewell!

GLOUCESTER *falls forward*

[*Aside*] And yet I know not how conceit may rob
The treasury of life when life itself
Yields to the theft. Had he been where he
      thought,
By this had thought been past. [*Aloud*] Alive, or
      dead?
Ho, you sir! friend! Hear you, sir? Speak!
[*Aside*] Thus might he pass indeed; yet he revives.
[*Aloud*] What are you, sir?

GLOUCESTER   Away, and let me die.

EDGAR Hadst thou been aught but gossamer,
      feathers, air,
(So many fathom down precipitating),   50
Thou'dst shivered like an egg; but thou dost
      breathe,
Hast heavy substance, bleed'st not, speak'st, art
      sound.
Ten masts at each make not the altitude
Which thou hast perpendicularly fell;
Thy life's a miracle. Speak yet again.

GLOUCESTER But have I fall'n, or no?

EDGAR From the dread summit of this chalky bourn.
Look up a-height; the shrill-gorged lark so far
Cannot be seen, or heard. Do but look up.

GLOUCESTER Alack, I have no eyes.   60
Is wretchedness deprived that benefit

[63] beguile   *trick (by committing suicide)*

[71] whelked   *twisted in a spiral*
     enridgéd   *corrugated with rippling waves*
[73] clearest   *purest*
[73–4] make . . . impossibilities   *are honoured for doing what men consider impossibilities*

[76–7] till . . . die   *until affliction itself gives up and dies*

[80] free   *unencumbered*
[81–2] The safer . . . thus   *the sounder sense (of Gloucester) will never adjust itself to finding Lear in this condition. Edgar is afraid that all he has done for Gloucester's self-control will be useless when he finds Lear raving mad. The entry of Lear in this scene, 'mad' as the Quarto says, is meant to be very startling. Edgar calls it a 'side-piercing sight'. Probably he is festooned with weeds, as Cordelia described him (IV. 4). A director must make sure that his appearance is enough to shock Edgar, who was with the King in the early stages of his madness.*
[83–4] they cannot . . . himself   *they cannot prosecute me for making counterfeit money; being the true king, my coinage is the true coinage (i.e. it is the others who are the false rulers)*
[86] Nature . . . respect   *the true king is better than the artificial ones (though Lear himself made the latter)*
[87] press-money   *money paid to a recruit*

To end itself by death? 'Twas yet some comfort
When misery could beguile the tyrant's rage
And frustrate his proud will.

EDGAR   Give me your arm.
  Up; so. How is't? Feel you your legs? You
    stand.

GLOUCESTER Too well, too well.

EDGAR   This is above all strangeness.
  Upon the crown o'th' cliff what thing was that
  Which parted from you?

GLOUCESTER   A poor unfortunate beggar.

EDGAR As I stood here below methought his eyes
  Were two full moons; he had a thousand noses,   70
  Horns whelked and waved like the enridgéd sea.
  It was some fiend. Therefore, thou happy father,
  Think that the clearest gods, who make them
    honours
  Of men's impossibilities, have preserved thee.

GLOUCESTER I do remember now. Henceforth I'll
    bear
  Affliction till it do cry out itself
  'Enough, enough,' and die. That thing you speak
    of,
  I took it for a man. Often 'twould say
  'The fiend, the fiend'; he led me to that place.

EDGAR Bear free and patient thoughts.

Enter LEAR, *mad*

                    But who comes here?   80
  The safer sense will ne'er accommodate
  His master thus.

LEAR No, they cannot touch me for coining; I am
  the king himself.

EDGAR O thou side-piercing sight!

LEAR Nature's above art in that respect. There's your
  press-money. That fellow handles his bow like a

[88] crow-keeper *boy paid to scare crows*

draw ... yard *draw your bow to the full extent of the arrow (which was a cloth-yard in length)*

[90] There's my gauntlet *He pretends to throw it down as a feudal challenge.*

prove it on *maintain my challenge against*

[91] brown bills *halberdiers*

[92] i' th' clout *on the target*

word *password*

[93] marjoram *a herb thought to cure diseases of the brain*

[97–8] told me ... were there *pretended I was old and wise before I was*

[98–9] To say 'ay' and 'no' to *to agree with*

[100] no good divinity *against the biblical injunction 'let your yea be yea and your nay nay' (James 5:12)*

[103] found 'em *found them out (as liars)*

[105] ague-proof *immune to a shivering fever*

[106] trick *characteristic manner*

[108] the subject *my subjects*

[109] cause *case against you*

[111] Die for adultery *Adultery was not a capital offence in Elizabethan times nor (as we gather from Gloucester's history) in the imagined period of the play. Lear has an Old Testament decree in mind, concerning which Christ said, 'He that is without sin among you, let him first cast a stone at her' (John 8:3–7).*

[114–16] for Gloucester's ... sheets *Married fidelity is meant to ensure and preserve good family relationships; but such 'kindness' was more to be seen in Gloucester's illegitimate son than my legitimately born daughters. There is therefore no point in not being promiscuous.*

[117] luxury *lust*

for ... soldiers *a population increase would enable Lear to have the bigger army he needs*

[118–23] *Having authorised promiscuity, Lear now 'argues' that chastity in women is only a façade, anyway.*

[119] forks *legs*

presages snow *promises chastity*

[120] minces virtue *primly parades her virtue*

[122] fitchew *polecat*

soiléd *lusty with feeding on fresh grass*

crow-keeper; draw me a clothier's yard. Look, look,
a mouse! Peace, peace; this piece of toasted cheese
will do't. There's my gauntlet; I'll prove it on a   90
giant. Bring up the brown bills. O, well flown, bird;
i'th' clout, i'th' clout: hewgh! Give the word.

EDGAR Sweet marjoram.

LEAR Pass.

GLOUCESTER I know that voice.

LEAR Ha! Goneril with a white beard? They flattered
me like a dog and told me I had the white hairs in
my beard ere the black ones were there. To say
'ay' and 'no' to everything that I said! 'Ay,' and 'no'
too, was no good divinity. When the rain came to 100
wet me once and the wind to make me chatter, when
the thunder would not peace at my bidding, there I
found 'em, there I smelt 'em out! Go to, they are not
men o' their words. They told me I was everything;
'tis a lie – I am not ague-proof.

GLOUCESTER The trick of that voice I do well
   remember:
Is't not the king?

LEAR   Ay, every inch a king!
When I do stare, see how the subject quakes.
I pardon that man's life. What was thy cause?
Adultery?   110
Thou shalt not die. Die for adultery? No!
The wren goes to 't, and the small gilded fly
Does lecher in my sight.
Let copulation thrive: for Gloucester's bastard son
Was kinder to his father than my daughters
Got 'tween the lawful sheets.
To 't, luxury, pell-mell! for I lack soldiers.
Behold yon simpering dame
Whose face between her forks presages snow,
That minces virtue and does shake the head   120
To hear of pleasure's name;
The fitchew nor the soiléd horse goes to 't

[124] centaurs   *i.e. lustful beasts*

[126] But . . . inherit   *the gods are in possession only as far as the waist*

[128–9] There's hell . . . consumption   *Lear turns away in disgust from his own invocation of sexual license. Women's sexuality destroys man physically and spiritually.*

[130] civet   *perfume (from the civet cat)*
      apothecary   *chemist*

[133] mortality   *human life – and death*

[135] so . . . naught   *in this way decay to nothing*

[136] I remember . . . enough   *Lear is aware (at some level and in some fashion) who Gloucester is and what must have happened to him. This powerful phrase includes the sense of remembering him as a man who had eyes and of asking himself why he should now be eyeless. Then he turns rapidly in what follows to associate Gloucester's sexual license with his eyelessness. (See the note on V. 3. 171–2.)*
      squiny   *squint*

[137] blind Cupid   *Cupid was often pictured blindfold; here Lear thinks of the picture as the sign of a brothel.*

[138] challenge   *See l. 90.*

[140] take . . . report   *believe this if I were told it*

[143] case of eyes   *eye-sockets*

[144] are . . . me?   *is that what you mean?*

[146] heavy case   *bad state*

[148] feelingly   *by touch, and with deep feeling*

[149] Art mad?   *Lear translates Gloucester as saying he has no understanding, only feeling.*

[151] simple   *low-born*

She scorns such actions, but goes to it (hypocrite)

With a more riotous appetite.
Down from the waist they are centaurs,
Though women all above.
But to the girdle do the gods inherit,
Beneath is all the fiend's.
There's hell, there's darkness, there is the
    sulphurous pit;
Burning, scalding, stench, consumption: fie, fie,
    fie, pah, pah!
Give me an ounce of civet; good apothecary, 130
sweeten my imagination. There's money for thee.

GLOUCESTER O, let me kiss that hand!

LEAR Let me wipe it first; it smells of mortality.

GLOUCESTER O ruined piece of nature! This great
    world
Shall so wear out to naught. Dost thou know me?

LEAR I remember thine eyes well enough. Dost thou
    squiny at me?
No, do thy worst, blind Cupid; I'll not love.
Read thou this challenge; mark but the penning
    of it.

GLOUCESTER Were all thy letters suns, I could not
    see.

EDGAR [*Aside*] I would not take this from report. It   140
    is,
And my heart breaks at it.

LEAR Read.

GLOUCESTER What, with the case of eyes?

LEAR O ho, are you there with me? No eyes in your
head, nor no money in your purse? Your eyes are in
a heavy case, your purse in a light; yet you see how
this world goes.

GLOUCESTER I see it feelingly.

LEAR What, art mad? A man may see how this world
goes with no eyes. Look with thine ears: see how 150
yon justice rails upon yon simple thief. Hark in

[152] handy-dandy   *the infant's game of guessing which hand an object is in (Lear probably holds his closed fists out)*

[157] image   *symbol*

[159] beadle   *parish constable*

[160] lash that whore   *Whores were whipped at the cart's tail through the streets.*

[162] usurer . . . cozener   *one who is himself guilty of cheating people by charging excessive interest is in the position of punishing the petty trickster ('cozener')*

[163] Through . . . appear   *the sins of the ragged poor are very visible, and they seem very bad*

[164–5] Plate . . . breaks   *money is like ,armour; the spear of justice breaks against it without hurting its owner*

[167] None . . . I say none   *everybody is a sinner, so no one has a right to call any one else an offender*

   able   *give legal power to (the supposed offenders)*

[168] Take . . . me   *accept these truths from me*

[169] glass eyes   *false eyes, rather than spectacles (often said to be meant here)*

[170] politician   *one who uses deceitful schemes to advance himself*

[173] matter and impertinency   *significant and irrelevant things*

[179] wawl   *wail*

[181] that   *because*

[182] this great stage   *This is the very common idea of the world is a stage on which we strut about playing our brief parts.*

   block   *mounting-block (?)*

[183] delicate stratagem   *neat scheme*

[184] in proof   *to the test*

thine ear: change places and, handy-dandy, which
is the justice, which is the thief? Thou hast seen a
farmer's dog bark at a beggar?

GLOUCESTER Ay, sir.

LEAR And the creature run from the cur? there thou
mightst behold the great image of authority – a dog's
obeyed in office.

Thou rascal beadle, hold thy bloody hand!
Why dost thou lash that whore? Strip thy own 160
 back;
Thou hotly lusts to use her in that kind
For which thou whipp'st her. The usurer hangs
 the cozener.
Through tattered clothes great vices do appear;
Robes and furred gowns hide all. Plate sin with
 gold,
And the strong lance of justice hurtless breaks;
Arm it in rags, a pigmy's straw does pierce it.
None does offend, none, I say none. I'll able 'em.
Take that of me, my friend, who have the power
To seal th'accuser's lips. Get thee glass eyes
And like a scurvy politician seem
To see the things thou dost not. Now, now, now,
 now! 170
Pull off my boots. Harder, harder! So.

EDGAR O, matter and impertinency mixed!
 Reason in madness!

LEAR If thou wilt weep my fortunes, take my eyes.
 I know thee well enough; thy name is Gloucester.
 Thou must be patient. We came crying hither;
 Thou know'st the first time that we smell the air
 We wawl and cry. I will preach to thee: mark!

GLOUCESTER Alack, alack the day! 180

LEAR When we are born, we cry that we are come
 To this great stage of fools. This' a good block!
 It were a delicate stratagem to shoe
 A troop of horse with felt. I'll put't in proof,

213

[185] stolen upon   *i.e. with the silent troop of horse*

[190] natural . . . Fortune   *born plaything of fortune*

[193] seconds   *supporters*
[194] this . . . salt   *a man must be made of salt to weep so many tears*

[197] Like . . . bridegroom   *Lear sees another meaning in 'die bravely', perform the sexual act well; there is a third meaning in 'bravely', finely dressed, and that leads to 'smug', neat, spruce.*

[200] there's life in't   *it's not all over yet*
        an   *if*

[204] the general curse   *universal affliction*
[205] twain   *Goneril and Regan*

[206] speed you   *may you prosper*

[207] toward   *imminent*
[208] sure, and vulgar   *certain, and commonly known*

And when I have stolen upon these son-in-laws,
Then kill, kill, kill, kill, kill, kill!

Enter a GENTLEMAN *with* ATTENDANTS

GENTLEMAN O here he is; lay hand upon him. Sir,
  Your most dear daughter—
LEAR No rescue? What, a prisoner? I am even
  The natural fool of Fortune. Use me well;   190
  You shall have ransom. Let me have surgeons;
  I am cut to th' brains.
GENTLEMAN   You shall have anything.
LEAR No seconds? All myself?
  Why, this would make a man a man of salt,
  To use his eyes for garden water-pots,
  Ay, and laying autumn's dust. I will die bravely,
  Like a smug bridegroom. What! I will be jovial.
  Come, come, I am a king, masters, know you that?
GENTLEMAN You are a royal one, and we obey you.
LEAR Then there's life in't. Come, an you get it, you 200
  shall get it by running. Sa, sa, sa, sa.
            [Exit running; ATTENDANTS *follow*
GENTLEMAN A sight most pitiful in the meanest
  wretch,
  Past speaking of in a king! Thou hast one
  daughter
  Who redeems nature from the general curse
  Which twain have brought her to.
EDGAR Hail, gentle sir!
GENTLEMAN   Sir, speed you. What's your
  will?
EDGAR Do you hear aught, sir, of a battle toward?
GENTLEMAN Most sure, and vulgar; every one hears
  that,
  Which can distinguish sound.
EDGAR   But, by your favour,
  How near's the other army?   210

[211–12] the main . . . thought *sighting of the main force is expected hourly*

[216] worser spirit *evil angel*
[217] Well pray you *you pray well*

[220] by . . . sorrows *taught by sorrows which I have known through suffering them myself*
[221] pregnant to *capable of*
[222] some biding *a place to stay in*

[223] benison *blessing*

[224] To boot, and boot *in addition, and for your advantage*
　　　proclaimed prize *a man for whose capture a reward has been publicly offered*
[225] framed *made*
[227] Briefly . . . remember *call your sins to mind (and pray for forgiveness) quickly*
[228] friendly *(because he wishes to die)*

[230] published *proclaimed*

GENTLEMAN Near, and on speedy foot; the main
  descry
  Stands on the hourly thought.

EDGAR   I thank you, sir;
  that's all.

GENTLEMAN Though that the queen on special cause
  is here,
  Her army is moved on.

EDGAR   I thank you, sir.

                              [*Exit* GENTLEMAN

GLOUCESTER You ever-gentle gods, take my breath ~~see pg 181~~
  from me;   *picking up*
  Let not my worser spirit tempt me again   *hope again,*
  To die before you please!   *more +ve*

EDGAR   Well pray you, father.

GLOUCESTER Now, good sir, what are you?

EDGAR A most poor man, made tame to Fortune's
  blows,
  Who by the art of known and feeling sorrows   220
  Am pregnant to good pity. Give me your hand;
  I'll lead you to some biding.

GLOUCESTER   Hearty thanks;
  The bounty and the benison of Heaven
  To boot, and boot!

                Oswald wants to kill G to put him in
              Enter OSWALD *favour c/ Corn wil)*

OSWALD   A proclaimed prize! Most happy!
  That eyeless head of thine was first framed flesh
  To raise my fortunes. Thou old unhappy traitor,
  Briefly thyself remember; the sword is out
  That must destroy thee.

GLOUCESTER   Now let thy friendly hand
  Put strength enough to't.

                          [EDGAR *interposes*

OSWALD   Wherefore, bold peasant,
  Dar'st thou support a published traitor? Hence,   230

                            217

[231–2] th' infection . . . thee *you are infected by his misfortune* (*sudden death*)

[233–40] *Edgar acts the peasant which Oswald has called him by assuming a stock 'dialect' – what we now call 'Mummerset'.*

[233] Chill *I will*

    cagion *occasion*

[235] gait *way*

[236] An chud *if I should*

    zwaggered . . . life *killed by swaggering talk*

[237] 'twould . . . vortnight *I should have been dead a fortnight ago*

[238–39] che vor' ye *I warrant you*

[239] ice *I shall*

    costard *head* (*literally, apple*)

    ballow *cudgel*

[242] pick your teeth *i.e. knock your teeth out*

    no matter . . . foins *I don't care about your fencing movements*

[247] Upon *among*

[248] serviceable *obsequiously diligent*

[250] badness *a bad person* (*i.e. his mistress*)

[254] deathsman *executioner*

[255] Leave *by your leave*

    wax *the seal*

[256] To know . . . hearts *we torture our enemies to get information*

[257] Their . . . lawful *it is more lawful to rip their correspondence*

[259] cut him off *murder Albany*

[259–60] want not *is not lacking*

[260] fruitfully offered *available in plenty*

[260–61] There . . . done *nothing will have been achieved*

ACT FOUR, SCENE SIX

Lest that th'infection of his fortune take
Like hold on thee. Let go his arm.

EDGAR Chill not let go, zir, without vurther cagion.

OSWALD Let go, slave, or thou di'st.

EDGAR Good gentleman, go your gait, and let poor
volk pass. An chud ha' bin zwaggered out of my life,
'twould not ha' bin zo long as 'tis by a vortnight.
Nay, come not near th'old man; keep out, che vor'
ye, or ice try whither your costard or my ballow be
the harder. Chill be plain with you.   240

OSWALD Out, dunghill!

                              [*They fight*

EDGAR Chill pick your teeth, zir. Come; no matter
vor your foins.

                              [OSWALD *falls*

OSWALD Slave, thou hast slain me. Villain, take my
purse:
If ever thou wilt thrive, bury my body,
And give the letters which thou find'st about me
To Edmund, Earl of Gloucester; seek him out
Upon the British party. O, untimely death! Death!

                              [*He dies*

EDGAR I know thee well – a serviceable villain,
As duteous to the vices of thy mistress
As badness would desire.

GLOUCESTER   What, is he dead?   250

EDGAR Sit you down, father; rest you.
Let's see these pockets; the letters that he speaks
of
May be my friends. He's dead; I am only sorry
He had no other deathsman. Let us see.
Leave, gentle wax; and, manners, blame us not:
To know our enemies' minds we rip their hearts;
Their papers is more lawful.   [*Reads the letter*
*Let our reciprocal vows be remembered. You have
many opportunities to cut him off; if your will want
not, time and place will be fruitfully offered. There* 260

Goneril will kill her husband, Albany,
because she sees him weak

[263–4] supply . . . labour   *take his place as a reward for your pains*

[267] indistinguished space   *immeasurable extent*
        will   *lust*

[270] rake up   *cover up*
        post unsanctified   *unholy messenger*
[271] in . . . time   *at the appropriate time*
[273] death-practised Duke   *Duke whose death has been plotted*

[275] stiff   *unyielding (to insanity)*
        vile   *(because unfriendly in remaining sane)*
[276] ingenious   *conscious*
[277] distract   *mad*

[279–80] woes . . . themselves   *woes will be forgotten in insane fantasies*

[282] *What happens to Oswald's body, which Edgar was going to bury in the sands? A body would normally be dragged off the stage by the killer in these circumstances.*

ACT FOUR, scene 7

Just before the armies meet, Lear awakens from a deep sleep into a new life. He is reunited with Cordelia and asks her forgiveness. One cycle of the play is completed, but there are more people involved in the action than Lear and Cordelia.

[3] measure   *means of measurement*
        fail me   *be too limited for me (to do enough)*
[5–6] All . . . so   *all that I have told is the simple truth, neither exaggerated nor curtailed, but as it happened (i.e. reward would be understandable if more had been claimed, or if more had been done)*

*is nothing done if he return the conqueror. Then am
I the prisoner, and his bed my gaol; from the loathed
warmth whereof deliver me, and supply the place for
your labour.*

> *Your (wife, so I would say) affectionate servant,*
> *Goneril*

O indistinguished space of woman's will!
A plot upon her virtuous husband's life,
And the exchange my brother! Here in the sands
Thee I'll rake up, thou post unsanctified   270
Of murderous lechers; and in the mature time
With this ungracious paper strike the sight
Of the death-practised Duke. For him 'tis well
That of thy death and business I can tell.

GLOUCESTER The King is mad; how stiff is my vile
    sense
That I stand up and have ingenious feeling
Of my huge sorrows! Better I were distract:
So should my thoughts be severed from my griefs,
And woes by wrong imaginations lose
The knowledge of themselves.   [*Drum afar off*
EDGAR   Give me your hand;   280
Far off methinks I hear the beaten drum.
Come, father, I'll bestow you with a friend.

> [*Exeunt*

Scene 7. *Enter* CORDELIA, KENT, *followed by* DOCTOR
and GENTLEMAN

CORDELIA O thou good Kent, how shall I live and
    work
To match thy goodness? My life will be too short,
And every measure fail me.
KENT To be acknowledged, madam, is o'er-paid.
All my reports go with the modest truth;
Nor more, nor clipped, but so.

[6] suited   *dressed*

[7] weeds   *clothes (his disguise as a servant)*

[9] shortens ... intent   *is too soon for what I have planned (see note to IV. 3. 52)*

[10] My ... it   *I ask it as a favour to me*

[11] meet   *fitting*

[16] wind up   *bring into tune (as with a stringed instrument)*

[17] child-changéd   *changed in nature by his children (?)*

[20] I' th' sway of   *as directed by*

[24] I ... temperance   *I am sure he will be calm*

[25] *The line is omitted in the Folio, which gives a stage direction for Lear to be carried in a chair by servants. It seems clear that origin-ally Lear was revealed in the recess at the back of the stage, and that in later years the staging was changed to that indicated in the Folio.*

[29] in thy reverence   *against thy revered person*

[30] flakes   *locks of hair*

CORDELIA   Be better suited;
  These weeds are memories of those worser hours;
  I prithee put them off.

KENT   Pardon, dear madam;
  Yet to be known shortens my made intent.
  My boon I make it that you know me not   10
  Till time, and I, think meet.

CORDELIA Then be't so, my good lord. [*To the*
  DOCTOR] How does the King?

DOCTOR Madam, sleeps still.

CORDELIA O you kind gods,
  Cure this great breach of his abuséd nature!
  Th'untuned and jarring senses, O, wind up
  Of this child-changéd father!

DOCTOR   So please your Majesty
  That we may wake the King? He hath slept long.

CORDELIA Be governed by your knowledge, and
    proceed
  I'th' sway of your own will. Is he arrayed?   20

GENTLEMAN Ay, madam; in the heaviness of sleep
  We put fresh garments on him.

DOCTOR Be by, good madam, when we do awake
    him;
  I doubt not of his temperance.

CORDELIA   Very well.

DOCTOR Please you draw near. – Louder the music
  there!

    Music. The DOCTOR *draws back curtains, and*
    reveals LEAR *asleep in a chair*

CORDELIA O my dear father, restoration hang
  Thy medicine on my lips, and let this kiss
  Repair those violent harms that my two sisters
  Have in thy reverence made!

KENT   Kind and dear princess!

CORDELIA Had you not been their father, these   30
  white flakes

[31] challenge *demand*

[33] deep . . . thunder *deep-voiced thunder with dreadful bolts*

[35] cross *forked*
perdu *sentry in exposed position at risk of his life*
[36] thin helm *his head*

[38] fain *constrained*

[40] short *broken up*
[41] at once *together*
[42] concluded all *come to a complete end*

[44] royal lord . . . your Majesty *While Lear was asleep, Cordelia addressed him as 'my dear father' (l. 26); when he is awake, he is her sovereign king.*
[45–8] *Lear thinks he is coming from the sleep of death to endure eternal punishment in hell, tied to a flaming wheel; Cordelia apears to him as a saved soul in heaven.*
[47] that *so that*

[53] abused *deluded*

[60] fond *silly*

Did challenge pity of them. Was this a face
To be opposed against the warring winds?
To stand against the deep dread-bolted thunder
In the most terrible and nimble stroke
Of quick cross lightning? To watch – poor
  perdu! –
With this thin helm? Mine enemy's dog,
Though he had bit me, should have stood that
  night
Against my fire; and wast thou fain, poor father,
To hovel thee with swine and rogues forlorn,
In short and musty straw? Alack, alack!   40
'Tis wonder that thy life and wits at once
Had not concluded all. He wakes; speak to him.

DOCTOR Madam, do you; 'tis fittest.

CORDELIA How does my royal lord? How fares your
  Majesty?

LEAR You do me wrong to take me out o'th' grave.
Thou art a soul in bliss; but I am bound
Upon a wheel of fire, that mine own tears
Do scald like molten lead.

CORDELIA   Sir, do you know me?

LEAR You are a spirit, I know; where did you die?

CORDELIA Still, still, far wide!   50

DOCTOR He's scarce awake; let him alone awhile.

LEAR Where have I been? Where am I? Fair
  daylight?
I am mightily abused; I should e'en die with pity
To see another thus. I know not what to say.
I will not swear these are my hands. Let's see;
I feel this pin prick. Would I were assured
Of my condition!

CORDELIA   O, look upon me, sir,
And hold your hand in benediction o'er me;
No, sir, you must not kneel.

LEAR   Pray do not mock me;
I am a very foolish fond old man,   60

[61] not . . . less   *This is nonsensically precise when applied to the vagueness of ' Fourscore and upward'; it illustrates the condition of Lear's mind.*

[65] mainly   *largely*

[71] Be . . . wet?   *can you really be crying?*

[77] abuse   *deceive*

[80] even o'er   *The meaning is uncertain, and the text may be corrupt. 'Go over' is the general sense required.*
[82] Till . . . settling   *until he is more settled*

[86] Holds it true   *is it confirmed as true*

[89] conductor   *leader*

Fourscore and upward, not an hour more nor less;
And, to deal plainly,
I fear I am not in my perfect mind.
Methinks I should know you, and know this man,
Yet I am doubtful; for I am mainly ignorant
What place this is; and all the skill I have
Remembers not these garments, nor I know not
Where I did lodge last night. Do not laugh at me,
For (as I am a man) I think this lady
To be my child Cordelia.

CORDELIA   And so I am, I am.   70

LEAR Be your tears wet? Yes, faith; I pray weep
    not.
  If you have poison for me, I will drink it;
  I know you do not love me, for your sisters
  Have (as I do remember) done me wrong;
  You have some cause; they have not.

CORDELIA   No cause, no cause.

LEAR Am I in France?

KENT   In your own kingdom, sir.

LEAR Do not abuse me.

DOCTOR Be comforted, good madam; the great rage,
    You see, is killed in him; and yet it is danger
    To make him even o'er the time he has lost.   80
    Desire him to go in; trouble him no more
    Till further settling.

CORDELIA Will't please your Highness walk?

LEAR You must bear with me. Pray you now, forget
    and forgive; I am old and foolish.

                [Exeunt all but KENT *and the* GENTLEMAN

GENTLEMAN Holds it true, sir, that the Duke of
    Cornwall was so slain?

KENT Most certain, sir.

GENTLEMAN Who is conductor of his people?

KENT As 'tis said, the bastard son of Gloucester.   90

GENTLEMAN They say Edgar, his banished son, is with
    the Earl of Kent in Germany.

[93] Report is changeable   *rumour varies. It is important that at the beginning of the scene the Gentleman should be talking to the Doctor well away from the conversation in which Kent talks to Cordelia in his own person.*

[95] arbitrement   *decisive encounter*

[97] My point . . . wrought   *my purpose and conclusion will be thoroughly worked out*

[98] Or well . . . fought   *whether my work has a good or a bad conclusion depends on the result of the day's fighting*

KENT Report is changeable. 'Tis time to look about;
the powers of the kingdom approach apace.
GENTLEMAN The arbitrement is like to be bloody.
Fare you well, sir.   [*Exit*
KENT My point and period will be throughly wrought,
Or well or ill, as this day's battle's fought.   [*Exit*

ACT FIVE, scene 1

The coming together of the forces opposing Lear and Cordelia is disturbed by the discord between Edmund and Albany, and by the rivalry between Goneril and Regan for Edmund's affection. A disguised Edgar makes his way into the enemy camp with a mysterious message, while his brother determines that Lear and Cordelia must not be allowed to remain alive.

[1] Know   *find out from*
   his last purpose   *his most recent plan*
[4] bring . . . pleasure   *tell me his definite intentions*
[5] Our . . . man   *Oswald*
   miscarried   *come to harm*
[6] doubted   *feared*

[9] honoured   *honourable*

[11] forfended   *forbidden*

[12] doubtful   *fearful*
[12–13] conjunct . . . hers   *coupled with her in the fullest intimacy*

[15] endure her   *allow her (to become intimate with Edmund)*

[16] Fear me not   *don't be afraid of what I shall do*

[22] rigour of our state   *harshness of our government*

ACT FIVE

Scene 1. *Enter, with drum and colours,* EDMUND, REGAN,
OFFICERS, *and* SOLDIERS

Albany is holding back, not wanted to commit, wrong

EDMUND Know of the Duke if his last purpose hold,
Or whether, since, he is advised by aught
To change the course. He's full of alteration
And self-reproving. Bring his constant pleasure.

                         [*Exit* OFFICER

REGAN Our sister's man is certainly miscarried.
EDMUND 'Tis to be doubted, madam.
REGAN   Now, sweet lord,
You know the goodness I intend upon you.
Tell me but truly – but then speak the truth –
Do you not love my sister?
EDMUND   In honoured love.
REGAN But have you never found my brother's way   10
To the forfended place?
EDMUND   That thought abuses you.
REGAN I am doubtful that you have been conjunct
And bosomed with her, as far as we call hers.
EDMUND No, by mine honour, madam.
REGAN I never shall endure her. Dear my lord,
Be not familiar with her.
EDMUND   Fear me not.
She and the Duke her husband!

       Enter, with drum and colours, ALBANY,
           GONERIL, SOLDIERS

GONERIL [*Aside*] I had rather lose the battle than
    that sister
Should loosen him and me.
ALBANY Our very loving sister, well be-met.   20
Sir, this I heard; the King is come to his
    daughter,
With others whom the rigour of our state

231

[25] It touches . . . land   *it concerns me in so far as there is an invasion by France*

[26–7] Not bolds . . . oppose   *The text seems corrupt here. The required sense is that Albany does not regard his action as an attack on the king, or others who are on the opposite side because of real grievances. If 'bolds' is correct, it must mean 'give support to' – the implication being that Albany does not think that supporting the King is treasonable.*

[28] you speak nobly   *Heavy sarcasm from Edmund.*

Why . . . reasoned?   *how can you reason thus? (i.e. make a distinction between opposing the French army and not opposing Lear and his allies)*

[30] particular broils   *private quarrels*

[32] ancient of war   *most experienced officers*

[33] presently   *immediately*

[36] convenient   *fitting*

[37] I . . . riddle   *I know the hidden meaning of what you say (i.e. that Regan is afraid Goneril will see Edmund)*

[40] this letter   *i.e. that which Oswald was taking from Goneril to Edmund*

[44] avouchéd   *declared*
     miscarry   *come to misfortune*

[45] of   *in*

[46] machination ceases   *evil plots cease so far as you are concerned*

Forced to cry out. Where I could not be honest,
I never yet was valiant. For this business,
It touches us as France invades our land,
Not bolds the King, with others whom, I fear,
Most just and heavy causes make oppose.

EDMUND Sir, you speak nobly.

REGAN   Why is this reasoned?

GONERIL Combine together 'gainst the enemy;
  For these domestic and particular broils   30
  Are not the question here.

ALBANY   Let's then determine
  With th'ancient of war on our proceeding.

EDMUND I shall attend you presently at your tent.

REGAN Sister, you'll go with us?

GONERIL No.

REGAN 'Tis most convenient; pray go with us.

GONERIL [*Aside*] O ho, I know the riddle. – I will
    go.

    As they are going out, enter EDGAR *disguised*

EDGAR If e'er your Grace had speech with man
    so poor,
  Hear me one word.

ALBANY   I'll overtake you.
                [*Exeunt all but* ALBANY *and* EDGAR
                                          Speak.

EDGAR Before you fight the battle, ope this letter.   40
  If you have victory, let the trumpet sound
  For him that brought it; wretched though I seem,
  I can produce a champion that will prove
  What is avouchéd there. If you miscarry,
  Your business of the world hath so an end,
  And machination ceases. Fortune love you!

ALBANY Stay till I have read the letter.

EDGAR   I was forbid it.
  When time shall serve, let but the herald cry,
  And I'll appear again.

[50] o'erlook   *scrutinise*

[53] diligent discovery   *careful reconnaissance*
[54] greet the time   *address ourselves to the circumstances*

[56] jealous   *suspicious*

[61] carry . . . side   *play out my part in the game (with Goneril)*

[63] countenance   *authority*
[64-5] Let her . . . taking off   *In her undelivered letter, Goneril had suggested Edmund should murder Albany. Edmund prefers to leave it to her.*
[65] taking off   *killing*
[68] Shall   *they shall*
        state   *position as Earl of Gloucester and potential husband of one of the rulers of England*
[69] Stands . . . defend   *requires positive action*

ACT FIVE, scene 2

The battle is fought, and the French army under Cordelia is defeated.

[Alarum]   *trumpet call for battle*
[1] father   *old man. Edgar has not revealed himself yet.*

ALBANY   Why, fare thee well.
  I will o'erlook thy paper.   [*Exit* EDGAR 50

Enter EDMUND

EDMUND The enemy's in view; draw up your powers.
  Here is the guess of their true strength and forces,
  By diligent discovery; but your haste
  Is now urged on you.
ALBANY   We will greet the time. [*Exit*
EDMUND To both these sisters have I sworn my love;
  Each jealous of the other, as the stung
  Are of the adder. Which of them shall I take?
  Both? One? Or neither? Neither can be enjoyed
  If both remain alive. To take the widow
  Exasperates, makes mad her sister Goneril;   60
  And hardly shall I carry out my side,
  Her husband being alive. Now then, we'll use
  His countenance for the battle, which being done,
  Let her who would be rid of him devise
  His speedy taking off. As for the mercy
  Which he intends to Lear and to Cordelia,
  The battle done, and they within our power,
  Shall never see his pardon; for my state
  Stands on me to defend, not to debate.   [*Exit*

Scene 2. *Alarum within. Enter, with drum and colours,*
LEAR, CORDELIA *holding him by the hand, and* SOLDIERS,
over the stage, and exeunt.

Enter EDGAR *and* GLOUCESTER

EDGAR Here, father, take the shadow of this tree
  For your good host. Pray that the right may thrive.
  If ever I return to you again,
  I'll bring you comfort.

[Retreat]   *trumpet call for a retreat*

[6] ta'en   *(taken) captured*

[8] a man . . . here   *this is as good a place to die as any*

[9–10] endure . . . hither   *accept without complaint the time appointed for their death, just as they must for their birth*

[11] Ripeness is all   *the ripe or proper time is everything. This phrase has behind it a whole philosophy of 'decorum', which is the desire that all one's actions should be wholly suited to and worthy of the time and the occasion.*

ACT FIVE, scene 3

In this concluding scene, Lear, defeated in war, is triumphant in his reunion with Cordelia, while the victory of the British forces turns literally to poison. With extraordinary medieval ceremony, Edgar takes his revenge on Edmund, but while it is being performed Cordelia is executed, and Lear loses the only thing that could keep him alive. As the play ends, Albany, Kent and Edgar turn away in weariness and sickness of heart.

[1] good guard   *let there be strict guard*

[2–3] Until . . . censure them   *until the more permanent decisions are made by those who are to pass judgement on them*

[4] meaning   *intention*

[10–11] When thou . . . forgiveness   *'Mutual forgiveness of each vice – such are the gates of Paradise' (William Blake).*

[13] gilded butterflies   *spruce courtiers*

poor rogues   *Courtiers busily talking of the latest developments at court are thought of by Lear as mere idlers and wastrels, doing nothing more useful than vagabonds ('rogues').*

GLOUCESTER   Grace go with you, sir!

[*Exit* EDGAR

Alarum and Retreat within

Enter EDGAR

EDGAR Away, old man; give me thy hand, away!
   King Lear hath lost, he and his daughter ta'en.
   Give me thy hand; come on!
GLOUCESTER No further, sir; a man may rot even
   here.
EDGAR What, in ill thoughts again? Men must
   endure
   Their going hence, even as their coming hither;   10
   Ripeness is all. Come on.
GLOUCESTER   And that's true too.

[*Exeunt*

Scene 3. *Enter in conquest with drum and colours,*
EDMUND; LEAR *and* CORDELIA *as prisoners*; SOLDIERS,
CAPTAIN

EDMUND Some officers take them away: good guard,
   Until their greater pleasures first be known
   That are to censure them.
CORDELIA   We are not the first
   Who with best meaning have incurred the worst.
   For thee, oppressèd King, I am cast down;
   Myself could else out-frown false Fortune's frown.
   Shall we not see these daughters and these sisters?
LEAR No, no, no, no! Come, let's away to prison.
   We two alone will sing like birds i'th' cage.
   When thou dost ask me blessing, I'll kneel down   10
   And ask of thee forgiveness. So we'll live,
   And pray, and sing, and tell old tales, and laugh
   At gilded butterflies, and hear poor rogues

= all religious words,
rear is penitent

237

[16] take upon 's *undertake the care of*
     mystery *hidden meaning*
[17] God's spies *Lear sees himself and Cordelia, with the knowledge he has so terrifyingly earned in madness and suffering, as in a special relationship with God as compared with worldly men still preoccupied with externals. They will not be spying on men, but they will be like soldiers in enemy country, with secret knowledge entrusted to them by God.*
     wear out *last longer than*
[18] packs and sects *groups and parties*
[20] sacrifices *the offering up of their lives in prison to the service of the gods (Lear returns to the plural, 'gods'.)*
[21] throw incense *i.e. show their approval*
[22] brand *burning piece of wood*
     from heaven *Only with God's consent could they be parted now.*
[23] like foxes *Foxes were driven out of their holes by fire and smoke.*
[24] good-years *The meaning of this is not known.*
     fell *skin*
[25] starved *perished (not specifically with hunger)*
[31-2] men . . . time is *men should bend themselves to the demands of the moment*
[33] become *go well with*
     Thy great employment *the great service you are being asked to do*
[34] question *discussion*

[36] write happy *declare yourself happy*

[37] carry *manage (see below, ll. 252-4)*

Talk of court news; and we'll talk with them too –
Who loses and who wins, who's in, who's out –
And take upon 's the mystery of things,
As if we were God's spies; and we'll wear out,
In a walled prison, packs and sects of great ones
That ebb and flow by th' moon.

EDMUND   Take them away.

LEAR Upon such sacrifices, my Cordelia,   20
    The gods themselves throw incense. Have I
        caught thee?
    He that parts us shall bring a brand from heaven
    And fire us hence like foxes. Wipe thine eyes;
    The good-years shall devour them, flesh and fell,
    Ere they shall make us weep! We'll see 'em
        starved first.
    Come.
                    [*Exeunt* LEAR *and* CORDELIA *under guard*

EDMUND Come hither, captain; hark.
    Take thou this note; go follow them to prison.
    One step I have advanced thee; if thou dost
    As this instructs thee, thou dost make thy way   30
    To noble fortunes. Know thou this, that men
    Are as the time is; to be tender-minded
    Does not become a sword. Thy great employment
    Will not bear question; either say thou'lt do't,
    Or thrive by other means.

CAPTAIN   I'll do't, my lord.

EDMUND About it; and write happy when th'hast
        done.
    Mark, I say instantly; and carry it so
    As I have set it down.

CAPTAIN I cannot draw a cart, nor eat dried oats;
    If it be man's work I'll do't.   [*Exit* 40

Flourish. Enter ALBANY, GONERIL, REGAN,
                SOLDIERS

239

[41] strain *disposition*

[45] merits *deserts*

[48] retention . . . guard *confinement under duly appointed guard*

[50] pluck . . . bosom *pull the hearts of the common people*

[51] turn . . . eyes *turn the weapons of those we have conscripted against us*

[57-8] the best . . . sharpness *the worthiest disputes are cursed by those who have suffered from them, before their ire has cooled. Edmund is playing for time while his commission against Lear and Cordelia is carried out, and this bland remark is little more than a vague suggestion that people are too worked up at the moment for justice to be done.*

[61] subject of *subordinate in*

[62] list *desire*

[66] immediacy *closeness*

[69] your addition *the titles you have given him*

ALBANY Sir, you have showed today your valiant
   strain,
  And Fortune led you well. You have the captives
  Who were the opposites of this day's strife;
  I do require them of you, so to use them
  As we shall find their merits and our safety
  May equally determine.

EDMUND   Sir, I thought it fit
  To send the old and miserable King
  To some retention and appointed guard;
  Whose age had charms in it, whose title more,
  To pluck the common bosom on his side
  And turn our impressed lances in our eyes
  Which do command them. With him I sent the
   Queen,
  My reason all the same; and they are ready
  Tomorrow, or at further space, t'appear
  Where you shall hold your session. At this time
  We sweat and bleed; the friend hath lost his
   friend;
  And the best quarrels, in the heat, are cursed
  By those that feel their sharpness.
  The question of Cordelia and her father
  Requires a fitter place.

Edmund sends for King as is only so Albany's rights

ALBANY   Sir, by your patience,   60
  I hold you but a subject of this war,
  Not as a brother.

Albany compliments him but states relation goes no further

REGAN   That's as we list to grace him.
  Methinks our pleasure might have been
   demanded
  Ere you had spoke so far. He led our powers,
  Bore the commission of my place and person
  The which immediacy may well stand up
  And call itself your brother.

GONERIL   Not so hot!
  In his own grace he doth exalt himself
  More than in your addition.

Quarrel of jealous rivals

241

[70] compeers *equals*
[71] the most *most clearly shown*

[75] From . . . stomach *with unabated anger*
    General *Edmund*
[77] the walls is thine *She is a fortress or a city surrendered to Edmund.*

[80] let-alone *prohibition*
    good will *consent*
[81] Half-blooded fellow *bastard*
[82] prove *by defending it in combat*

[83] hear reason *Albany pretends to urge discussion rather than combat, but is in fact about to produce the reason for there being no marriage.*
[84] in thy attaint *as a sharer in your disgrace*

[87] sub-contracted *there being already a main contract with him*

[90] bespoke *engaged*
    interlude *little play*

[94] make it *make it good*

[95] in nothing *in no respect*

REGAN   In my rights
  By me invested, he compeers the best.   70

ALBANY That were the most if he should husband
  you.

REGAN Jesters do oft prove prophets.

GONERIL   Holla, holla!
  That eye that told you so looked but asquint.

REGAN Lady, I am not well, else I should answer
  From a full-flowing stomach. General,
  Take thou my soldiers, prisoners, patrimony;
  Dispose of them, of me; the walls is thine.
  Witness the world that I create thee here
  My lord and master.

GONERIL   Mean you to enjoy him?

ALBANY The let-alone lies not in your good will.   80

EDMUND Nor in thine, lord.

ALBANY   Half-blooded fellow, yes.

REGAN [*To Edmund*] Let the drum strike, and prove
  my title thine.

ALBANY Stay yet; hear reason. Edmund, I arrest thee
  On capital treason, and, in thy attaint,

                   [*Pointing to* GONERIL

  This gilded serpent. For your claim, fair sister,
  I bar it in the interest of my wife;
  'Tis she is sub-contracted to this lord,
  And I, her husband, contradict your banns.
  If you will marry, make your loves to me;
  My lady is bespoke.

GONERIL   An interlude!   90

ALBANY Thou art armed, Gloucester; let the
  trumpet sound.
  If none appear to prove upon thy person
  Thy heinous, manifest, and many treasons,
  There is my pledge. [*Throwing down a glove*] I'll
  make it on thy heart,
  Ere I taste bread, thou art in nothing less
  Than I have here proclaimed thee.

[97] medicine   *i.e. poison*

[99] villain-like   *like a serf*

[104] single virtue   *unassisted valour*

[110] of quality or degree   *The challenger must be of high position.*

[111] lists   *registers*

REGAN   Sick, O sick!

GONERIL [*Aside*] If not, I'll ne'er trust medicine.

EDMUND There's my exchange. [*Throwing down a
       glove*] What in the world he is
That names me traitor, villain-like he lies.
Call by the trumpet; he that dares approach,   100
On him, on you – who not? – I will maintain
My truth and honour firmly.

ALBANY A herald, ho!

EDMUND   A herald, ho, a herald!

ALBANY Trust to thy single virtue, for thy soldiers,
All levied in my name, have in my name
Took their discharge.

REGAN   My sickness grows upon me.

ALBANY She is not well; convey her to my tent.

                           [*Exit* REGAN, *led away*

                    Enter a HERALD

Come hither, herald. Let the trumpet sound,
And read out this.   [*A trumpet sounds*

HERALD [*Reads*] If any man of quality or degree 110
within the lists of the army will maintain upon
Edmund, supposed Earl of Gloucester, that he is a
manifold traitor, let him appear by the third sound
of the trumpet. He is bold in his defence.

                           [*First trumpet*
Again!   [*Second trumpet*
Again!   [*Third trumpet*

          Trumpet answers within. Enter EDGAR *armed,*
                  a TRUMPETER *before him*

ALBANY Ask him his purposes – why he appears
Upon this call o'th' trumpet.

HERALD   What are you?
Your name, your quality, and why you answer
This present summons?

                                              245

[121] canker-bit   *worm-eaten*

[123] cope   *encounter*

[128] it   *to draw it against a traitor*
[128–9] honours . . . profession   *i.e. as a knight*
[129] protest   *solemnly declare*
[130] Maugre   *in spite of*
[131] fire-new   *freshly forged*
[132] heart   *courage*
[134] Conspirant   *conspirator*

[135] upward   *top*
[136] descent   *lowest part*
[137] toad-spotted   *covered in infamy, as the poisonous toad is covered with spots*
[139] whereto I speak   *He speaks direct to the heart of his foe.*

[140] In wisdom . . . name   *in case his opponent is of base birth. Having been dubbed Earl of Gloucester, Edmund has become very attentive to the niceties of rank and blood which were made so much of in the rules of combat.*
[142] say   *(assay) proof*
[143] safe and nicely   *safely, by being punctilious*

[146] hell-hated   *hated as hell is hated*
[147] for they yet glance by   *because the treasons and the lie which I return to you only glance off you*

[150] Save him   *spare his life*

EDGAR   Know my name is lost,   120
  By treason's tooth bare-gnawn and canker-bit;
  Yet am I noble as the adversary
  I come to cope.
ALBANY   Which is that adversary?
EDGAR What's he that speaks for Edmund, Earl of
    Gloucester?
EDMUND Himself. What say'st thou to him?
EDGAR   Draw thy sword,
  That, if my speech offend a noble heart,
  Thy arm may do thee justice; here is mine.
  Behold, it is the privilege of mine honours,
  My oath, and my profession. I protest,
  Maugre thy strength, place, youth, and eminence,   130
  Despite thy victor-sword and fire-new fortune,
  Thy valour and thy heart, thou art a traitor,
  False to thy gods, thy brother, and thy father,
  Conspirant 'gainst this high illustrious prince,
  And, from th'extremest upward of thy head
  To the descent and dust below thy foot,
  A most toad-spotted traitor. Say thou no,
  This sword, this arm, and my best spirits are bent
  To prove upon thy heart, whereto I speak,
  Thou liest.
EDMUND   In wisdom I should ask thy name;   140
  But since thy outside looks so fair and warlike,
  And that thy tongue some say of breeding
    breathes,
  What safe and nicely I might well delay
  By rule of knighthood, I disdain and spurn.
  Back do I toss these treasons to thy head,
  With the hell-hated lie o'erwhelm thy heart,
  Which, for they yet glance by and scarcely bruise,
  This sword of mine shall give them instant way
  Where they shall rest for ever. Trumpets, speak!
                [*Alarums. They fight.* EDMUND *falls.*
ALBANY Save him, save him!

247

   practice *deceitful contrivance*

[153] cozened *deceived*

[154] this paper *i.e. her letter to Edmund*
   Hold, sir *spoken to Edgar (?)*

[157–8] the laws . . . arraign me *Goneril blusters in the anger of her frustration: 'I'm the ruler, and I'll do what I like'.*
[158] arraign *bring to judgement*

[160] govern *restrain*

[164] if . . . noble *i.e. if this has been a fair combat between equals in rank*
[165] exchange charity *forgive each other*

[169] pleasant *pleasure-giving*

[171–2] The dark . . . eyes *i.e. the dark vice of Gloucester's adultery with Edmund's mother has earned the dark punishment of his blindness. Contrast this severe view of Edmund's conception with Gloucester's jocose attitude in the opening lines of the play.*
[173] The wheel . . . here *Edmund not only accepts Edgar's grim belief in divine punishment, but extends it. He is the fruit of the adultery, and in his destruction the sin is fully repaid. See Introduction, pages 21–22.*
[174] gait *movement and posture*

GONERIL   This is practice, Gloucester: 150
   By th' law of war thou wast not bound to answer
   An unknown opposite: thou art not vanquished,
   But cozened and beguiled.

ALBANY   Shut your mouth, dame.
   Or with this paper shall I stop it. – Hold, sir. –
   Thou worse than any name, read thine own evil.
   No tearing, lady! I perceive you know it.

GONERIL Say if I do; the laws are mine, not thine;
   Who can arraign me for't?

ALBANY   Most monstrous! O!
   Know'st thou this paper?

GONERIL   Ask me not what I know. [*Exit*

ALBANY Go after her; she's desperate; govern her.   160
                    [*Exit an* OFFICER

EDMUND What you have charged me with, that have
     I done,
   And more, much more; the time will bring it out;
   'Tis past, and so am I. But what art thou
   That hast this fortune on me? If thou'rt noble,
   I do forgive thee.

EDGAR   Let's exchange charity.
   I am no less in blood than thou art, Edmund;
   If more, the more th'hast wronged me.
   My name is Edgar, and thy father's son.
   The gods are just, and of our pleasant vices
   Make instruments to plague us: 170
   The dark and vicious place where thee he got
   Cost him his eyes.

EDMUND   Th'hast spoken right, 'tis true.
   The wheel is come full circle; I am here. *wheel of Fortune*

ALBANY [*To* EDGAR] Methought thy very gait did
     prophesy
   A royal nobleness; I must embrace thee;
   Let sorrow split my heart if ever I
   Did hate thee or thy father.

EDGAR   Worthy prince, I know't.

[180] List   *listen to*

[183–5] life's sweetness . . . at once   *how sweet life is that we'd rather undergo the pain of death each hour than die once and for all*

[187] habit   *dress*

[188–9] rings . . . stones   *The eye-sockets are seen as ornamental rings without their jewels.*

[195] flawed   *cracked*

[198] smilingly   *It was the grief that had cracked his heart; the contrary pressure of a sudden surge of joy was too much for him, but it was with his new happiness that he died.*

[202] dissolve   *in tears*

[203] period   *terminating point*

[204–6] but another . . . extremity   *to describe yet another grief in full detail would be too much, and would go beyond the most extreme limit*

[207] big in clamour   *loudly lamenting (the death of his father)*

[210] endured   *suffered*

ALBANY Where have you hid yourself?
  How have you known the miseries of your father?
EDGAR By nursing them, my lord. List a brief tale;   180
  And when 'tis told, O that my heart would burst!
  The bloody proclamation to escape
  That followed me so near (O, our life's sweetness,
  That we the pain of death would hourly die,
  Rather than die at once!) taught me to shift
  Into a madman's rags, t'assume a semblance
  That very dogs disdained; and in this habit
  Met I my father with his bleeding rings,
  Their precious stones new lost; became his guide,
  Led him, begged for him, saved him from   190
    despair;
  Never (O fault!) revealed myself unto him
  Until some half hour past, when I was armed.
  Not sure, though hoping, of this good success,
  I asked his blessing, and from first to last
  Told him our pilgrimage. But his flawed heart
  (Alack, too weak the conflict to support)
  'Twixt two extremes of passion, joy and grief,
  Burst smilingly.
EDMUND   This speech of yours hath moved me,
  And shall perchance do good. But speak you on;
  You look as you had something more to say.   200
ALBANY If there be more, more woeful, hold it in;
  For I am almost ready to dissolve,
  Hearing of this.
EDGAR   This would have seemed a period
  To such as love not sorrow; but another,
  To amplify too much, would make much more,
  And top extremity. Whilst I
  Was big in clamour, came there in a man,
  Who, having seen me in my worst estate,
  Shunned my abhorred society; but then, finding
  Who 'twas that so endured, with his strong arms   210
  He fastened on my neck and bellowed out

[215] puissant   *powerful*
   strings of life   *heart strings. These were thought of as real tendons or ligaments supporting the heart and necessary to life. Kent has had a fatal seizure and is dying.*
[217] tranced   *unconscious*
[219] enemy king   *king who declared himself an enemy by banishing him*

[Enter . . . bloody knife]   *For five lines the audience is held in suspense not knowing who is dead; an obvious thought is that it is Cordelia.*

[222] smokes   *steams*

[228] Now marry   *This union in death is the only solution to the problem which Edmund had explained at V. 1. 57–8.*

[233] very   *mere*

As he'd burst heaven; threw him on my father;
Told the most piteous tale of Lear and him
That ever ear received, which in recounting
His grief grew puissant and the strings of life
Began to crack. Twice then the trumpets sounded,
And there I left him tranced.

ALBANY   But who was this?

EDGAR Kent, sir, the banished Kent, who in disguise
Followed his enemy king and did him service
Improper for a slave.   220

Enter a GENTLEMAN, *with a bloody knife*

GENTLEMAN Help, help! O help!

EDGAR   What kind of help?

ALBANY   Speak, man!

EDGAR What means this bloody knife?

GENTLEMAN   'Tis hot, it smokes;
It came even from the heart of – O, she's dead!

ALBANY Who dead? Speak, man!

GENTLEMAN Your lady, sir, your lady! And her
    sister   *Goneril has poisoned Regan*
By her is poisoned; she confesses it.

EDMUND I was contracted to them both; all three
Now marry in an instant.

EDGAR   Here comes Kent.

Enter KENT

ALBANY Produce the bodies, be they alive or dead;
                              [*Exit* GENTLEMAN
This judgement of the heavens, that makes us
    tremble,   230
Touches us not with pity. [*Seeing* KENT] O, is this
    he?
The time will not allow the compliment
Which very manners urges.

[234] aye   *for ever*

[235] of us   *by us*

[237] object   *spectacie*

[238] Yet . . . beloved   *This note of pride, so incongruous here, throws a shaft of light on the insecurity below the surface of Edmund's self-assurance.*

[254] fordid   *destroyed*
[255] The gods defend her!   *See Introduction, pages 18, 20.*

KENT   I am come
  To bid my king and master aye good night.
  Is he not here?

ALBANY   Great thing of us forgot!
  Speak, Edmund; where's the king? and where's
     Cordelia?

  The bodies of GONERIL *and* REGAN *are brought out*

  See'st thou this object, Kent?

KENT Alack, why thus?

EDMUND   Yet Edmund was beloved. *[shows she is conceited]*
  The one the other poisoned for my sake,
  And after slew herself.   240

ALBANY Even so. Cover their faces.

EDMUND I pant for life. Some good I mean to do,
  Despite of mine own nature. Quickly send   *[wants to show*
  (Be brief in it) to th' castle, for my writ   *repentance by*
  Is on the life of Lear and on Cordelia.   *saving Lear]*
  Nay, send in time!

ALBANY   Run, run, O run!

EDGAR To who, my lord? [*To* EDMUND] Who has
     the office? Send
  Thy token of reprieve.

EDMUND Well thought on. Take my sword,
  Give it to the captain.

ALBANY   Haste thee, for thy life!   250
                              [*Exit an* OFFICER

EDMUND He hath commission from thy wife and me
  To hang Cordelia in the prison and
  To lay the blame upon her own despair,
  That she fordid herself.

ALBANY The gods defend her!
  Bear him hence awhile.

                              [EDMUND *is borne off*

  Enter LEAR *with* CORDELIA *dead in his arms,*
          followed by the OFFICER

                                                          255

[257] men of stones   *men made out of stones, not flesh and blood*

[258] Had I . . . eyes   *'eyes' here are for seeing as well as weeping. 'If I were in your place, seeing what you see, my tongue would lament and my eyes would weep, so that,' etc.*

[259] She's . . . ever   *At some point during this speech, perhaps before he says this, Lear lays Cordelia's body on the ground, but continues to support her head.*

[262] stone   *specular stone, a translucent mineral used for glass*

[263] Is this the promised end?   *Kent has all along worked towards the moment when, with Lear once again accepting Cordelia, he would reveal himself to the master who had banished them both (see IV. 3. 52–5; IV. 7. 9, 97–8). But the phrase in which he asks himself, in utter misery, if this is the conclusion which all has been leading to, immediately suggests the wider question, whether this is the end of the world, which is how Edgar takes it. See Introduction, page 19.*

[264] Fall and cease   *let the heavens fall and life cease*

[266] redeem   *cancel out*

[276] falchion   *curved sword*

[278] crosses spoil me   *troubles worsen my skill with a sword*

[280–81] If Fortune . . . behold   *if Fortune were to boast of two people, as the best examples of what her love and her hate could do, the example of her hate would be Lear*

[282] This . . . sight   *I can't see clearly (?)*

LEAR Howl, howl, howl! O, you are men of stones!
  Had I your tongues and eyes, I'd use them so
  That heaven's vault should crack! She's gone for
  ever.
  I know when one is dead, and when one lives;   260
  She's dead as earth. Lend me a looking-glass;
  If that her breath will mist or stain the stone,
  Why, then she lives.

KENT   Is this the promised end?

EDGAR Or image of that horror?

ALBANY   Fall and cease!

LEAR This feather stirs – she lives! If it be so,
  It is a chance which does redeem all sorrows
  That ever I have felt.

KENT [Kneeling]   O my good master!

LEAR Prithee away!

EDGAR   'Tis noble Kent, your friend.

LEAR A plague upon you, murderers, traitors all!
  I might have saved her; now she's gone for ever!   270
  Cordelia, Cordelia, stay a little. Ha?
  What is't thou say'st? Her voice was ever soft,
  Gentle and low, an excellent thing in woman.
  I killed the slave that was a-hanging thee.

OFFICER 'Tis true, my lords, he did.

LEAR   Did I not, fellow?
  I have seen the day, with my good biting falchion
  I would have made them skip; I am old now,
  And these same crosses spoil me. Who are you?
  Mine eyes are not o' th' best, I'll tell you straight.

KENT If Fortune brag of two she loved and hated,   280
  One of them we behold.

LEAR This is a dull sight. Are you not Kent?

KENT   The same:
  Your servant Kent. Where is your servant Caius?

LEAR He's a good fellow, I can tell you that;
  He'll strike, and quickly too. He's dead and rotten.

KENT No, my good lord; I am the very man –

[287] I'll...straight   *I'll attend to that without delay. Lear is not listening. Kent's long-postponed revelation is a failure*

[290] Nor ... else   *In completing what he was saying before, Kent's words come to have a second meaning as an answer to Lear's welcome: no one is welcome at such a scene as this.*

[291] fordone   *destroyed*

[292] desperately   *in a state of despair*

[294] bootless   *fruitless*

[297] this great decay   *Usually said to refer to Lear, this more probably means the wretched general situation they now find themselves in.*

[301] boot   *addition*

addition   *title*

[305] my poor fool   *There is something inexpressibly poignant in Lear's using this endearment for Cordelia at this point. His tenderness seems all the greater for gently using a disparaging term like this. And she is a fool, fooled by fortune, or the gods. He also brings back to our minds the Fool, long since disappeared from the play, who is the only other person he has seemed to love.*

[309] this button   *at his throat, as he feels an increasing sense of suffocation*

[310] Do you see this? . . look there!   *It is for the actor to decide whether he is to show Lear, at the moment of his death, thinking that Cordelia is still alive, and so dying with joy in his heart, or whether he will make Lear end without false hope, asking the others to look on this inexplicable and unalterable fact, that Cordelia is dead. It is a crueller play if Lear is shown dying in a misapprehension that her lips have moved, and that she is alive. It is a greater play, perhaps, if we accept, as J. K. Walton has argued, that Lear dies in full recognition of what has happened.*

LEAR I'll see that straight.

KENT That from your first of difference and decay
    Have followed your sad steps –

LEAR   You are welcome hither.

KENT Nor no man else. All's cheerless, dark, and   290
    deadly.
    Your eldest daughters have fordone themselves,
    And desperately are dead.

LEAR   Ay, so I think.

ALBANY He knows not what he says, and vain is it
    That we present us to him.

EDGAR   Very bootless.

Enter a MESSENGER

MESSENGER Edmund is dead, my lord.

ALBANY   That's but a trifle here.
    You lords and noble friends, know our intent:
    What comfort to this great decay may come
    Shall be applied. For us, we will resign,
    During the life of this old majesty,
    To him our absolute power; [*To* EDGAR *and* KENT]   300
    you to your rights,
    With boot and such addition as your honours
    Have more than merited. All friends shall taste
    The wages of their virtue, and all foes
    The cup of their deservings. O see, see!

LEAR And my poor fool is hanged! No, no, no life!
    Why should a dog, a horse, a rat have life,
    And thou no breath at all? Thou'lt come no more,
    Never, never, never, never, never!
    Pray you, undo this button. Thank you, sir.
    Do you see this? Look on her! Look – her lips!   310
    Look there, look there!

EDGAR   He faints. My lord my lord!

KENT Break, heart; I prithee break.

EDGAR   Look up, my lord.

[313] ghost *spirit*
      pass *to a life beyond death*
[314] rack *the instrument of torture*

[317] usurped *wrongfully held possession of*

[323] The weight . . . obey *we must not try to escape from the*
burdens of the situation
[324] ought to say *i.e. some formal or consoling sentence*

260

KENT Vex not his ghost. O, let him pass. He hates
   him,
   That would upon the rack of this tough world
   Stretch him out longer.

                              [LEAR *dies*

EDGAR   He is gone indeed.
KENT The wonder is he hath endured so long;   *introduces*
   He but usurped his life.   *extrimities to*
                                               which Lear has
                                               suffered
ALBANY Bear them from hence. Our present
   business
   Is general woe. [*To* KENT *and* EDGAR] Friends of
   my soul, you twain
   Rule in this realm, and the gored state sustain.   320
KENT I have a journey, sir, shortly to go. *he wants to*
   My master calls me; I must not say no. *die*
EDGAR The weight of this sad time we must obey;
   Speak what we feel, not what we ought to say.
   The oldest hath borne most; we that are young
   Shall never see so much, nor live so long.

        [*Exeunt, with a dead march, bearing the bodies of*
                        LEAR *and his three daughters*

Shakespeare Interviews

devised, written and directed by Robert Tanitch

Four tapes, each of which contains a brief introduction to one of Shakespeare's most popular plays, followed by a searching interview with the main characters in the play. The actions and motives of the characters, and the conflict and drama of their relationships are revealed through the interviewer's skilful questioning.

Shakespeare Interviews can be enjoyed both at a simple and a sophisticated level. For the student coming to Shakespeare for the first time, these tapes will be invaluable in helping him to overcome the initial language barrier. For the student of Shakespeare at CSE, O and A level who is familiar with the play which he is studying, these tapes offer a stimulating approach, and a springboard for new ideas.

Characters interviewed:
Macbeth : Macbeth, Lady Macbeth
Julius Caesar : Brutus, Cassius, Julius Caesar, Mark Antony
Hamlet : Hamlet, Ophelia, Polonius, Claudius, Gertrude
Romeo and Juliet : Romeo, Juliet, Mercutio, Friar Lawrence, the Nurse

Macbeth	open reel 333 15111 9	cassette 333 15373 1
Julius Caesar	open reel 333 15112 7	cassette 333 15375 8
Hamlet	open reel 333 15113 5	cassette 333 15376 6
Romeo and Juliet	open reel 333 15114 3	cassette 333 15377 4

Themes

identity (human worth)
father - children
one should follow heart
order of nature
fate